Praise for Katrina Nguy

"If you ever doubt if the American Dream is still alive, if miracles still happen, if wonderful people are still out there doing amazing things, and if God is still working through seemingly ordinary people, read *Live to Give*. You'll enjoy an epic story of overcoming and faithfully moving forward as told by Katrina. And you'll feel a spark of possibility that much more remains possible in your life."

—*John O'Leary, #1 national bestselling author of* On Fire

"Dr. Nguyen's book highlights the art of human interaction and its power to make a connection between two seemingly unrelated people. *Live to Give* is heartwarming and made me realize the true difference kindness can make. It empowers me to be compassionate with others, especially my patients as a psychiatrist."

—*Jenny Tumba, MD*

"This is such an amazing message of God's faithfulness to us. How He has a bigger plan for us, if we just give ourselves over to him. Katrina's examples of how she uses the strengths the Lord has given her to be a blessing are so inspiring! This has definitely made me evaluate my relationship with God and if I truly am putting Him first in all areas of my life."

—*Kerstein Bracken, RN, CCRN*

"I believe everyone in life thinks they can do more, professionally, personally or both. We all struggle with this notion in one way or another, and this idea was really brought home to me after reading the last chapter in *Live to Give*. It made me realize that life really is too short, and what you do for others on a daily basis really matters. I always thought that there is no greater feeling than helping someone else in any way possible. Katrina's book really solidifies that mindset for me. Her book should make us all reexamine our purpose in life and ask ourselves, are we really doing enough to inspire and touch the lives of the people around us."

—*Roy Dubash, MD*

"As a single mother of a special needs child, it is difficult to find that someone who has this type of impact on your child and helps in every way possible. It is great to know there are people out there that have this type of drive and heart. Katrina Nguyen is that person and I am happy to know her. She is a fabulous human being and we need more people like her."

—*Annalisa White, CMA*

"*Live to Give* reminds me that there are always ways to give back. Even if the task seems small to me, it could mean the world to someone else. It makes me strive to be a better person today than I was yesterday."

—*Nicole Bleile, RN, BSN*

"Knowing Katrina, I am not surprised by her reaction [to people in need]. Her heart is generous and she is always looking for ways to be of service to others in need. Katrina touches the lives of those around her with her spirit by showing us how we, too, can help. I am blessed by knowing her."

—*Teresa Surrett, LPN*

"Those looking in from the outside do not always see the real sacrifices of those in medicine. It is difficult, you give up many things to study and learn what is needed to be successful, and then this carries into your career, some of the same sacrifices. That is how some are wired—to give of themselves to improve the lives of others. Professionally, it reminds me of the dedication it has taken and continues to take every day."

—*Karen Martin, RN, BSN*

Live to Give

*An inspirational memoir about
freedom, faith, and selflessness*

Kim-Doan Katrina Nguyen, MD

Pediatric Gastroenterologist

Founder of Faithful-2-Fitness, NFP

HILTON PUBLISHING • CHICAGO, ILLINOIS

Hilton Publishing Company
5261-A Fountain Drive
Crown Point, IN 46307
219-922-4868
www.hiltonpub.com

Copyright © 2020 by Kim-Doan Katrina Nguyen
ISBN 978-0-9777779-8-3

Notice: The information in this book is true and complete to the best of the author's and publisher's knowledge. This book is intended only as an information reference and should not replace, countermand, or conflict with the advice given to readers by their physicians. The author and publisher disclaim all liability in connection with the specific personal use of any and all information provided in this book.

All rights reserved. No part of this book may be reproduced or transmitted in any form or by any means, electronic or mechanical, including photocopy, recording, or any information storage or retrieval systems, including digital systems, without written permission from the publisher, except by a reviewer who may quote brief passages from the book in a review.

Angela Vennemann, Senior Editor and Design
Megan Lippert, Executive Vice President, Hilton Publishing Division

Library of Congress Cataloging-in-Publication Data has been applied for.

Contents

Preface   7

Introduction   9

1.   Sowing The Seeds Of Faith And Culture   13

2.   An Education In Science   29

3.   Embarking On A Medical Career   33

4.   A Tiger Joins The Tigers   42

5.   Pediatric Gastroenterology Fellowship   50

6.   My First Real Job   57

7.   My Second Real Job   60

8.   The Formation Of Faithful-2-Fitness   62

9.   Light Of The World Retreat And Faith Community   69

10. The People Who Shaped Me   72

11. Giving Without Judging   93

12. Why Live To Give   113

To Pete and Angie Scordato:

Best wishes and God bless!
Katrina Nguyen
[signature]

Preface

It was December 2013 and I had just returned home from California after celebrating my parents' sixtieth wedding anniversary. It was such an unexpectedly emotional experience and it inspired me to keep working on this memoir. The time with my family once again emphasized the uniqueness of our family dynamics which allow all nine of my siblings and I to have special bonds even though we may be thousands of miles apart.

For me, writing this memoir served many purposes. It gave me an opportunity to document my family's experiences so that future generations can learn about their ancestors. I never knew any of my grandparents, so I want my nieces and nephews to know their roots. I hope to share how my Vietnamese heritage combined with my Catholic upbringing has shaped so many aspects of my life, including my "live to give" philosophy. I also hope that this will be a chance for those who grew up with us to understand who we are as individuals, not just a person in "that family with two Catholic priests." What are people's perceptions of who we are compared to who we really are? This memoir is my attempt to provide a bird's-eye view of our family, which has often been perceived as perfect and ideal but is tainted with the problems and struggles that every family endures. By sharing our experiences, I hope to help families who are struggling with similar issues.

Introduction

I AM THE EIGHTH OF ten children born into a Vietnamese Catholic family. My father was a fisherman who made daily treacherous trips to the open sea in a small boat in order to make a living and raise a family. My mother was a simple housewife who had been orphaned by the time she was seven years old. She lived with relatives and worked as a maid until she got married. Neither of my parents received any formal education.

About one month before the fall of Saigon, when I was fourteen months old, the province where my family lived (formerly known as Binh Tuy, now named Ham Tan) was attacked with artillery by the Communist army coming from the north. My parents abandoned our house, left behind all they owned, and began a dangerous journey with their children, then numbering eight, to escape the Communists, using only the small fishing boat that my father owned. Our family traveled by sea, dodging artillery fire and bombs. The stench of decaying dead bodies floating alongside our boat was constantly present. My siblings were exhausted, hungry, and thirsty throughout the journey. After days on the water, my family reached a temporary safe haven in a coastal province of Vietnam about 200 kilometers from our village called Vung Tau. However, the turmoil and fear was constant. There was chaos from hundreds of thousands of Vietnamese people trying to escape villages that were being attacked. Robberies, murder, and other crimes were happening on a regular basis. My family members lived with anxiety because my parents did not know what to do if that safe haven also came under attack.

On April 30, 1975, the Communist regime took over Saigon after the retreat of South Vietnam and United States forces, ultimately ending the war. My dad decided to take a leap of faith in order for our family to have a chance for survival. With our entire family on board, he took the small fishing boat into the ocean in the hopes that once we made it out into open waters, we would be rescued by humanitarian foreign ships. There was just a sliver of hope, and at times this hope dimmed when our fragile boat was tossed around in the turbulent waves under the stormy dark skies.

After three days and three nights, my parents saw a huge floating flat with thousands of people already on board. My dad decided we had to abandon our boat, but in order for all of us to board the crowded flat, we couldn't bring our belongings. We left behind everything except for ten bags of instant noodles and three gallons of water. We spent two days and two nights on the floating flat, which was being towed by three merchant ships towards international waters. There were more than 5,000 people on the flat and barely any standing room. With so many people on board, there were sanitation problems, and people had no choice but to relieve themselves wherever they were standing.

My family members witnessed people fighting while on the flat, trying to be the first to be rescued by humanitarian ships. Hundreds of people fell into the sea. Children, including babies, were crushed to death under the broken barricades that fenced in the flat, which had been used by the United States to transport weaponry. Blood trickled by the feet of my family members. My parents told my siblings not to fight to be rescued but to wait with confidence that God would bring the rescuers to us in His own time. My parents wanted the entire family to stay together and not to be separated into groups such as the elderly, men, women, or children. Because of this, my family was the last to leave the flat and board a merchant ship. By the time we boarded the ship, we had already run out of noodles and water. We had to search through the garbage that was left behind by other people who had already left the flat in order to find food for everyone in the family. My oldest brother, Hien, was so thirsty that he drank fish sauce because he was hallucinating that it was water.

After traveling on the merchant ship for two days and two nights, we arrived in the Philippines at U.S. Naval Base Subic Bay, where we began paperwork to be processed as refugees. A couple of days later, our family was transported by a C-130 airplane to Andersen Air Force Base in Guam. That was May 8, 1975.

My youngest sister, Mylene, was born in 1976 while we were staying in Guam. We eventually moved to New Orleans, Louisiana, where my youngest brother, Derek, was born in 1978. In 1980, we moved to California, where many of my family members still reside.

The Communist government, which took over all of Vietnam after April 1975, did not believe in religious freedom. Many Catholic leaders were not allowed to preach, celebrate Mass, or administer religious sacraments without the approval of the government leaders. Those caught violating these rules were arrested and imprisoned for spreading "anti-Communist propaganda." My family was Catholic and several of my brothers were in the seminary studying to become priests prior to the end of the Vietnam War. Several of our relatives had served in the South Vietnamese military, battling the spread of communism alongside the American military. Because of my family's political and religious affiliations, we were a prime target for persecution by the new Communist regime. Although we were forced out of our homeland due to our political and religious beliefs, I consider my family more fortunate than many other Vietnamese refugees. We all fled together and we have been blessed with many opportunities to fulfill our personal and professional goals.

On paper, the Communist government preaches socialism, but in reality the economy in Vietnam would not survive without capitalism being put into practice. Many people we know who have gone to Vietnam to "do business" have been deceived by the Communist government there. After paying for their land, property, and businesses, the government will later tell these people that what they paid for is still government property. There is no guarantee that contracts signed will actually be honored. There is so much corruption that is not reported about the Vietnamese Communist government. There is bribery that happens the moment anyone lands at the airport in Vietnam. The more you pay the bag screeners, the more you get to bring into the country. When people send boxes of gifts to their relatives in Vietnam, government workers will open up the boxes and take all the expensive things and then send what's left to the recipient, leaving the boxes partially opened as a blatant display that it has been tampered with. I pray that the U.S. government does not allow socialism to take root because socialism is the way communism will make its way into this country.

My parents often shared stories about how I beat the odds many times early in my life. I am the fifth girl in my family, which according to Vietnamese cultural beliefs is a sign of good fortunes to come. My parents said that when I was born, my father's fishing business in Vietnam flourished. However, I nearly died during my family's flight from the Communist regime to America. I almost fell into the ocean while being transferred from the flat to the merchant ship that was rescuing Vietnamese refugees. After surviving that ordeal, I became so ill in a refugee camp in Guam that my relatives had already prepared a burial site for me. Every time I heard stories like these, I became more convinced that God had a greater purpose for me in this life. He offered me many second chances in order for me to give other people their second chances in the future.

After many years of training in the medical field and encountering many opportunities to help people, I have decided to share how my life has become a journey with increasing emphasis on the phrase "live to give." I personally feel that many people who enter the medical field truly want to help people. Yet, many of us in the medical field tend to lose the passion to help others by the time we complete our training. Many of us get lost in chasing money, titles, homes, cars, hobbies, and a luxurious lifestyle. Don't get me wrong: all of that is a great reward for all the hard work we have put in to accomplish our goals. However, some of us often become fixated on fulfilling our desires to the point that we become blind to other people's basic needs. I am often frustrated watching how difficult it is to ask physicians to contribute to charitable causes. I often think to myself that if only everyone contributed a little bit of their time, talent, or treasure, then we could have a big impact on many of the world's problems. I hope that by sharing my life's journey I can inspire more people to take time to reflect on the numerous ways they can help others out of the kindness of their hearts, not because it is part of their job description. I have made it a habit every day to pray for God to help me fulfill His purpose for me in this world. Most of all, I ask God to help me to recognize ways I can help those less fortunate than me.

A fellow physician once told me that he admired my natural compassion for people. He said that compassion is not something he could teach me, but he believed that the more I practiced it, the greater it would become. I believe that although each of us is given different talents from our Creator, if we surround ourselves with people with loving hearts, we will be touched with a desire to help others using the gifts we have been given.

I frequently reflect on my mortality and one thing I know for sure. When the time comes for me to leave this world, I would like to be remembered as one who lived to give. As I share my life story, I hope you will see how the kindness of others and God's blessings in my life have inspired me to constantly seek out ways I can help people.

1

Sowing the Seeds of Faith and Culture

EARLY CHILDHOOD

Living in Louisiana

MY FIRST MEMORY OF MY childhood was growing up in Versailles, Louisiana, outside of New Orleans. Many of our relatives had settled in Versailles after coming from Guam or one of the Southeast Asian refugee camps. Versailles gradually became populated by Vietnamese people—around 500 at the time we arrived—so many religious services were celebrated in Vietnamese. The local Catholic church had catechism classes and Masses in Vietnamese. In addition to Masses, the Vietnamese families also organized many cultural celebrations to honor God, the Virgin Mary, and many Catholic saints who helped them during their journey to America.

Though I learned to speak Vietnamese from my parents, I learned to read and write in Vietnamese by attending catechism classes at the church in the afternoons, following my mornings at the "American school." Two nuns were in charge of these classes. One of the nuns, Sister Ngao, was older and more strict than the other one. There is a belief in Vietnamese culture that left-handedness is bad luck or evil, so Sister Ngao would use a small wooden stick to slap the palm of anyone who wrote with their left hand. She would dictate Vietnamese sentences to us, which we scribed and turned in at the end of class. If we were a few minutes late to class, we were not allowed to participate in the lesson and had to sit at the front facing the rest of the class until the lesson was over. Students learned quickly to come on time or not come at all. But despite her strict discipline, I am grateful to Sister Ngao. Because of her, I am able to fluently read, write, and speak Vietnamese even though I was only one year old when I arrived in the United States.

One of the ways I kept up with my Vietnamese language as I grew up in America was by helping my dad write letters to his siblings who still lived in Vietnam. Even though my dad could read, write, and converse well in the Central Vietnamese dialect, he was not as well-versed in formal Vietnamese language as other men his age. So when my dad wanted to write to his siblings in Vietnam, he would either dictate sentences for me to scribe or paraphrase his thoughts for one of my sisters, who would then write the letters. I learned the meaning and spelling of new words each time I wrote a letter for my dad, which expanded my Vietnamese vocabulary. My parents also subscribed to Vietnamese Catholic magazines, which I read to expand my vocabulary and improve my fluency, and my parents played all types of Vietnamese music at home. I learned to appreciate all genres of Vietnamese music, some of which my friends thought were better suited for old people. Topics that are common in Vietnamese music are love, war, and love & war.

Many of my friends who were much older than me when they immigrated to the United States are often surprised to know that I am fluent in Vietnamese. Most Vietnamese people think that those who came to the United States in 1975 or earlier would have "lost their roots." Thanks to my parents, even my youngest sister and brother, who were born in the United States, still have a great understanding and appreciation for the Vietnamese language and culture.

Refugees like my family members are grateful for freedom, education and employment opportunities in order to rebuild a life that we had lost after escaping our war-torn country. Our goal from the beginning of our refugee experience is for future generations to become productive citizens of the United States, be less dependent on help from the government, and to give back to the community. By succeeding and giving back, we honor those who helped us in our early days as refugees in the United States. We constantly learn the American history, language and culture. We constantly work on assimilation and proudly became U.S. citizens, continuing to pay our fair share of taxes and following the laws that govern this country. We embrace our freedom and opportunities in this country and never take it for granted.

As a physician, I am required to provide care to all patients regardless of their legal status, race, gender, ethnicity, religious affiliation, socioeconomic status, and political beliefs. So when I share my thoughts about illegal and legal immigration, I don't have a bias as to who I would provide care for in my office. I believe that every country has its rights to write and enforce laws in order to ensure the safety, security and prosperity of its own people. I have seen many physicians and scientists waiting for years to get a green card so that they can secure a job in the U.S. after extensive training. I don't think it's fair for people who come here illegally to suddenly get special legal status ahead of hard working professionals I mentioned above. I believe that people with talent should be considered for legal immigration and everyone who seeks asylum should go through the process legally, no matter how long it takes. It has been reported in the media that many illegal immigrants exploit children to seek asylum. Many have been involved in drugs, gang activity and other crimes. The vetting process for asylum consideration may take a long time, but it must be thorough in order to minimize the risk of bringing criminals into the United States. My heart aches when I hear stories of families who have been affected by crimes committed by illegal immigrants.

Living in Louisiana was great for cultural identity purposes but difficult for assimilation into American culture. Since the town gradually became more and more Vietnamese after the arrival of refugees, most of our family friends were Vietnamese. We wanted to learn English but only spoke it at school. We were encouraged to spend time with relatives instead of hanging out with friends. My siblings spent their free time playing Chinese jump rope and marbles, while typical American pastimes like going to the movies or baseball games were not even on our radar, either because of affordability or anxiety in such social settings. Being born into one culture and raised alongside another made it difficult for me to find my identity early on in life, but I have learned to embrace both cultures as I have gotten older.

My father worked in grocery stores with duties such as stocking and packing things. He also went on fishing trips with my uncles to catch fish that they could sell to neighbors and acquaintances. My siblings would help my parents sell the fish to make a little extra money to pay rent and bills. My mother worked sporadically along with other Vietnamese women, cleaning seafood such as oysters, clams, and shrimp for grocery stores. My older siblings had to coordinate their classes in junior high and high school so that at least one of them was available to babysit the younger siblings in case my mom got called into work. As refugees with lots of children, my parents were dependent on the government for assistance, but all the children in the family worked hard with the goal that one day we would be able to support ourselves. We strove for the day that we had careers that would allow us to give back to society in the same way we were helped during our early years in the United States.

Being a family of immigrants, we grew up for a short time relying on government assistance, something I used to be ashamed of. I was often fearful that one of my friends would see my mom shopping with food stamps. My mom was also like the extreme coupon shopper who could leave a store with groceries either for free or almost nothing. This type of shopping could be embarrassing because it held up the line. It was horrifying when my mom realized she wasn't getting a deal and decided to return half the stuff in the cart.

When I lived on my own, I realized the value of a penny. I understood how my mom was able to raise all ten of her kids by stretching that dollar without making us feel like we would starve. We always got what we needed, not what we wanted. My husband often tells me that he married me because I wasn't high-maintenance and was very practical. I prefer to get something like a laptop rather than perfume, flowers, or chocolates on special occasions. I don't care if I receive a birthday, anniversary, or Christmas gift from him. I value that we have dinner together on those occasions. Those are values that my parents definitely instilled in me.

Even though my husband and I each earn six-figure salaries, we are not lavish spenders, but we are also not stingy. We enjoy treating our family members. We want them to enjoy the fruits of our labor because our family members once took care of us. They are the ones who nurtured us so that we could earn the life we have today. Maybe they didn't contribute financially to our journey towards a career in medicine, but they were definitely praying for us every step of the way. Through the tough times, our family members believed in us.

My family's refugee experience in the United States—having to rebuild our lives from nothing—is what drives me to help the poor as often as I am capable. I ask God to help me recognize these opportunities to help my neighbors, to not turn a blind eye, and to never forget where I came from in the first place. Without the generosity of people who sponsored my family from refugee camps, none of us would be as accomplished as we are today. Stories that I hear about the kindness of those who helped us gain our footing in America are what reminds me to be kind to everyone I meet. Giving my time, talent, or treasures to those less

> *My family's refugee experience in the United States—having to rebuild our lives from nothing—is what drives me to help the poor as often as I am capable.*

fortunate than I am is my way of paying it forward.

I had school anxiety as early as in preschool and continuing through first grade. I didn't want to get on the school bus each morning. My mom and siblings who walked me to the school bus couldn't understand why my younger sister, Mylene, just hopped right onto the bus each morning while they had to drag me kicking-and-screaming. They were concerned that I would not make it very far in school with this attitude toward education so early in life.

This is the earliest photo of me, taken in kindergarten.

I attended Sherwood Forest Elementary School from kindergarten to first grade in New Orleans. My teacher was gorgeous, but I don't recall her name. I learned many nursery rhymes like "Hickory Dickory Dock," "Jack and Jill," and "Humpty Dumpty." I was good at memorizing but not so great at speaking English at the time. One day, I needed to use the bathroom so I raised my hand, walked up to the teacher, and pointed to the bathroom pass. I took the pass and rushed to the bathroom, which was pitch dark. I fumbled around but couldn't find the lights or the toilet seat. I rushed right back to ask for help, but the teacher was in the middle of a lesson, and I didn't want to interrupt her. So I sat down with all my might, trying not to urinate. The embarrassment came when I couldn't hold it in anymore and urinated all over myself and the floor. The teacher had to call my parents to pick me up after she loaned me a pair of jeans. Needless to say, I was horrified, which made going to school the next day even more difficult.

Another challenge my parents faced with me attending school was that I was frequently worried that teachers would take things away from me. I had a favorite jacket, for instance, that I never wanted to take off when I got to school. The teacher had to call my mom every day to have me remove my jacket. I also didn't like nap time in preschool and kindergarten, so either I would refuse to lie down on the floor mat or refuse to close my eyes. My mom thinks I was concerned that something would happen to me if I fell asleep outside of our home.

A memory that makes my sisters and I laugh every time has to do with a Vietnamese traditional dress called *ao dai*. In Vietnamese culture, *ao dai* is worn for special occasions such as weddings, New Year celebrations, church, temple or festivals. In Vietnam, *ao dai* is routinely worn by young girls going to school every day. The colors usually correlated with the woman's age—lighter colors for younger girls and darker colors for older women. It is worn with black, white, or matching colored pants. When I was in first grade, one of my aunts had bought me an *ao dai* and she asked me to come over to her house to get fitted. I was so excited to have an *ao dai*, so when it fit perfectly I kept it on and rushed home, not realizing that I only had underwear below the dress and not the long pants that are supposed to cover my buttocks and legs. My sisters and mom had such a good laugh when I entered the house. To this day, we still laugh about this and joke with anyone who puts on an *ao dai* to not forget their pants.

The Move to California

In 1980, my family moved to Orange County in California. It was difficult to leave the comfort of our Vietnamese community in New Orleans. However, it was a decision that was encouraged by my oldest brother Hien, who had been studying to become a priest in the Diocese of San Jose in northern California. Hien had been living there since September 1976 after leaving Guam. He saw many more educational opportunities for his siblings in California and believed that it would help our family assimilate better to American culture. My parents wanted to move to a city in California where there was a Vietnamese community, and my father also wanted to be near the ocean. These were the reasons why my brother decided Orange County would be the ideal place for us.

We took the Amtrak train because we could not afford plane tickets for twelve people. It was the longest road trip I've ever been on, but one of the most memorable. We often look at old photos and laugh at our odd hairstyles and mismatched pieces of clothing. We made it to California after several days and eventually rented a house in Garden Grove located on Sungrove Circle. It was the only house we could find whose owner was willing to rent to a family our size. The front yard was lined with small bushes, a rose bed, and many tall pine trees. Inside, there were two bathrooms and four bedrooms. One of the bedrooms had a window with a crack the size of a bullet hole right in the middle of the glass panel. The glass was shattered in a star-like projection from the hole, which had been duct-taped to hold the window together. There was a big combined living room and dining room that led to a large backyard surrounded by a tall, faded-pink brick wall.

One of our next door neighbors had two dogs that were constantly barking. His backyard had a pool and jacuzzi. He and his family were very nice and invited us over to go swimming often. Little did he know that we were all afraid of dogs, so during our first time over to his house, we dashed for the pool and jacuzzi when he let his dogs out to roam the backyard. I still recall that it was getting cold and our skin was getting pruney, but we waited until he locked up the dogs before we all got out of the pool and headed home. After he learned that we were afraid of dogs, he always locked up the dogs before we came over. My family became very good friends with this neighbor and we looked out for each other's houses when either of our families was not home.

At the time that my family moved to the house on Sungrove Circle, Hien was still in the seminary studying to become a Catholic priest. He had exposure to seminarian life in Vietnam and had been an altar server from the time he was twelve years old. He was eventually sponsored by the Diocese of San Jose to complete his training for the priesthood. He had many friends who were priests and nuns, and they were often invited to our home whenever he came home for vacation. My family recalled many occasions when these "holy people" would visit us and all of a sudden the entire house had a foul odor. My sisters would grab the lemon-scented Wizard spray in an attempt to cover up the odor, but the more they sprayed, the more pungent the foul odor became. Without fail, once the "holy people" left, the foul odor disappeared. We became very suspicious that something strange had occurred at this house. We asked the landlord many questions about this observation. All we found out that years ago there was gang activity in the area, which may have accounted for the bullet-shaped hole on the bedroom window. The landlord did not know any other details.

One morning, my mom was in the kitchen preparing lunch for my second oldest brother, Tuan, to take to work. She always prayed the Rosary while cooking. All of a sudden, she heard a creaking noise near the door to the garage. She thought the creaking noise was strange since my family closed and locked all doors to the house before going to bed. So my mom walked towards the garage door and saw that it was ajar. She closed and locked it again, but within a few minutes it was creaking again. My mom was too frightened to check if the door had opened again. She thought, How could it be creaking if it wasn't opened again? There was nobody else awake but my mom, so nobody else could have opened that door. She was quite puzzled and she mentioned it briefly to Tuan when he woke up for work, but neither of them dwelled on this strange occurrence.

A few weeks later, my family was sleeping soundly at night and did not hear any disturbances. We woke up the next morning to find that the pine trees in our front yard, which were about ten to twelve feet tall, had been wrapped in toilet paper all the way to the top. There were no signs that anyone climbed the roof or used a ladder to cause such a mess. All of the rose bushes and small shrubs were also covered in toilet paper. There were no signs of foul play, graffiti, or gang activity. None of the neighbors had heard any noise and none of their homes were desecrated in any way. The neighbors were scared for us but also quite puzzled. For several hours, all of us pitched in to clean up.

A few weeks after this incident, my mom was again praying and cooking in the kitchen one morning. This time, she heard the garage door creak open, saw a shadow come from the garage, pass the kitchen, and then disappear. She thought she was imagining, but then the garage door swung fully open on its own. She ran into the bedroom and woke everyone up. She showed us that the garage door was open and couldn't explain how that could have happened. All of us had a feeling that something eerie had occurred in this home, especially when we put together the foul odor, the toilet-paper incident, and the noises and shadows coming from the garage.

Soon after these strange occurrences, my family moved out. Many years later, we learned that other renters who lived at the house on Sungrove Circle experienced similar paranormal activities. We found out from other people that there was a former tenant who had committed suicide in the garage of that house, so I guess my mom's observations were not her imagination after all. I don't know whatever happened to that house, but to this day, my siblings and I still have chills when we talk about the house on Sungrove Circle.

My family moved into a two-bedroom apartment in another part of Garden Grove. The girls slept with Mom in one bedroom while the boys slept with Dad in the other room. There was one bathroom to share between all of us, so some of us showered at night while others showered in the morning. Even with twelve of us living there, we learned to share the bathroom and still give each other privacy.

I don't recall the name of the elementary school I attended while living on Sungrove Circle. I don't think I even completed a whole year at that school before we moved. When we moved, we ended up in a neighborhood in Garden Grove that consisted of mainly Vietnamese people. There was a mix of "gang-bangers" along with many practicing Catholic youth. My siblings and I joined either the church choir or the Eucharistic Youth Group at St. Barbara Catholic Church. My parents wanted us to assimilate to American culture and contribute our talents to our community and church as best we could. These activities also helped us keep up with Vietnamese culture and language.

Growing up in Orange County, I was immersed in a large Vietnamese Catholic community. Even before my brothers were ordained Catholic priests, spirituality was always an important part of my life. My siblings and I participated in church-related activities, everything from the Eucharistic Youth Group to the Legion of Mary to the church choir. We discovered our talents and made contributions to the parish however we could.

Once Hien and Huy were ordained Catholic priests, many of the nuns in our community would come over to our house to meet us. It was often an opportunity for them to recruit one of the girls to join the convent. Because I was one of the more soft-spoken and introverted ones in my family, many people thought I would be a good candidate to join the convent. Even after I came back home during breaks from medical school, some nuns were still trying to recruit me. I've always felt uncomfortable about religious people recruiting young people. I think that if there is "a calling from God," then it should be a personal epiphany between God and the individual. I think both of my brothers experienced that calling on their own and still remain committed to fulfilling their duties.

During my childhood, I went through the usual catechism classes and the sacraments as the appropriate time came. Religion to me seemed to involve a lot of rituals. My parents woke us up every morning at 6:00 a.m. to pray together. As the saying goes, a family that prays together stays together. My parents, especially Mom, really believed in this saying and reminded my siblings after they got married to keep that practice going. No matter what we had in store for the day, God and prayer always came first. We also prayed before bedtime. Sometimes, my parents would wait for us to come home from school to pray together, no matter how late it was. We went to church and sat together as a family. We were expected to be prim and proper and to dress appropriately for Mass, so my parents were understandably distressed and ashamed when Derek went through a rebellious period during which he had orange-dyed shaved hair. The rituals, daily prayers, and all the expected behaviors at church was what I knew about the practice of Catholicism while I was living at home.

My parents wanted us to keep the routine of going to school, going to youth groups or choir, and going to church. Education was the main focus for each of us, so my parents didn't want anything to distract us from this goal. They didn't let any of the girls work except during the summer if they weren't attending summer school. One of my brothers, Huy, took a third-shift job at Shakey's Pizza when he started college to help my family make ends meet. My parents were very apprehensive about him working because they were concerned that making money might make Huy lose focus on school.

We didn't have many social activities or toys, and not much time to watch TV. We played badminton or Chinese jump rope in the front yard that was shared with the entire apartment complex. But we couldn't go out and play until all homework was completed, we had folded the laundry, and helped prepare dinner. We participated in talent shows with the Eucharistic Youth Group and that was how many of us discovered our hidden talents in singing, music, drama, and artistic creativity. These skills continued to develop as we matured and learned to use our talents to develop a career or as part of volunteer activities.

This is how we stayed away from the gangster life, while around us we saw girls getting pregnant out of wedlock and boys getting shot because of their involvement in gang activities. We lived next door to a family who had many kids in gangs, and they would play loud music until 2:00 a.m. every day, with no regard for other people. We were afraid to confront them for fear of being hurt. We learned many years after we had moved away that a young man who used to live there had been shot by a restaurant owner in Westminster during an attempted robbery. Even though we shared one wall of our apartment with the family of gang members, my parents managed to keep us out of trouble.

While living in the two-bedroom apartment in Garden Grove, I attended Cook Elementary School. I walked home each day with some friends and often stopped by a liquor store to buy different types of candy for less than a quarter. I wore retainers at that time but loved to eat Now and Later candies, which were sour and stuck to your teeth like Tootsie Rolls. These sticky candies were not something I was supposed to be eating while I had retainers. One day, I came home with my mouth wide open and could barely swallow my saliva. My mom realized I had eaten a Now and Later, which made my lower retainer pop up. The piece of candy was stuck on the retainer and caused the retainer to pop off my lower teeth. My mom called the dentist's office, who had a driver pick me up for an appointment. The dentist put my retainer back in place, where it stayed for a few more years.

That was one dental visit where I couldn't tell the dentist that I didn't eat candy.

In 1983, we moved to Orange, California, into a three-bedroom apartment, with nine kids sharing the apartment with our parents. This neighborhood was ethnically diverse including Asians, Hispanics, Caucasians, and African Americans. I would consider it a low-income neighborhood and there was petty theft activity on a weekly basis. While my family was at church one Saturday evening, someone broke into the apartment and stole some electronics and jewelry. Luckily nobody was harmed since everyone was at church. We reported the incident to the police, but we never found out who did it.

I attended California Elementary School and made lots of friends, but still felt like I bonded more with the Vietnamese students. I don't recall being in an English as Second Language (ESL) program at California Elementary School but may have been placed in ESL classes at some point before then. My third grade teacher, Mrs. Mallard, treated me like a teacher's pet. I did very well in spelling so she asked me to help her grade spelling tests. There was one girl named Kelly Smart who started bullying me for my spelling homework because she didn't like that I was the teacher's pet. She copied my homework and threatened to hurt me if I told anyone. She followed me home after school to make sure I didn't meet with any teachers. She went from bullying me for spelling homework to making me meet her at the kindergarten classroom gates so she could copy most of my homework. I thought it was ridiculous that a white person was copying my English homework. At first, I thought she couldn't read, but I later realized she was just doing it out of laziness and to feel empowered. I don't know what ever happened to Kelly Smart, but I don't recall her being in my fourth grade class. To this day, I still think how ironic it was that her last name was Smart.

I won the school handwriting contest in fourth and fifth grades. I competed at the district level and felt so blessed just to see the inside of the Orange Unified School District building. Back then, it felt like I was visiting the White House. I didn't win the district competition, but it was an honor just to represent my school each of those years.

Something special happened in sixth grade. At California Elementary School, there were only two sixth-grade classrooms. One was taught by Mrs. Crum and the other by Mrs. Kempf. I was in Mrs. Kempf's class. There was a spelling bee every year; each sixth-grade class held their own spelling bee, and the top winners of each class were entered into the school spelling bee. I was among a handful of students that had made it to the school competition. I still recall spelling the winning word, "superintendent," and beating Matthew George, who was one of the smartest, nicest, and most conscientious students in the school. He was from Mrs. Crum's class and I didn't realize until I won what a big deal it was for Mrs. Kempf. It was the first time in the history of the school spelling bee that Mrs. Kempf's class won. She was so proud of me and I became one of her favorite students.

Mrs. Kempf knew how much I wanted to learn, so she told me about cheap books I could buy at the school book fair and helped me find interesting library books. I asked her how I could check out some encyclopedia volumes, so she found a way for me to borrow one volume at a time. I remember thinking that I wanted an encyclopedia set for Christmas. I devoured any books I got to borrow or buy. I checked out so many books one afternoon that I had to ask my sister Tatiana to come over from the neighboring Yorba Middle School to help me carry them home. I sweated so much as I carried all the books in my backpack; my family thinks that all of those books weighing me down caused me to become the shortest member of my family. My sister just couldn't believe how much I wanted to read. I would stay up until midnight studying while the rest of the family was sound asleep. My mom would wake up and say, "Why are you still awake? How are you going to get up tomorrow?" I suppose old habits don't die easily—I am still an avid reader and a night owl.

Yorba Middle School

At the end of sixth grade, I took a variety of tests that eventually placed me in the GATE (Gifted and Talented Education) program beginning in seventh grade. This meant that I would be enrolled in honors or Advanced Placement courses from seventh grade through twelfth grade. This was a personal challenge because I had no siblings who could help me when I had difficult assignments. Without any help from family members, I learned to be an independent learner and thinker. I devoted much of my holiday breaks and summer vacations to doing extra homework, while most of my closest friends were doing the bare minimum to advance to the next grade level. Towards the end of eighth grade, I participated in a science enrichment program in which college professors gave science lectures and demonstrated experiments on the weekends. This sparked my interest in science and I began to think seriously about pursuing a career in that field.

Around the same time, I learned about a summer job training program available to students who had completed eighth grade. I was granted a work permit through the school superintendent, and in June 1988 I was assigned to work at the Orange County Fire Department in the Records Department under the supervision of Lucille Mello, someone who came to be an important mentor to me. I quickly learned many clerical skills such as answering phone calls, handling the switchboard, intercom paging, typing, computer skills, filing, copying, faxing, and using the microfiche machine. I also had the opportunity to walk through the room where 911 dispatchers were answering calls. That experience enhanced my curiosity for a health care-related career path because I wanted to save lives. Even though I was only earning minimum wage, I learned to appreciate the hard work it took to earn a dollar and I devoted as many hours as I could to my job. I ended up working for Lucille each summer until 1990, after which I shifted my focus toward summer courses at Rancho Santiago College.

Lucille Mello

Lucille Mello was my first boss and remains a friend. She was the first person who gave me a glimpse of what it took to become successful. At fourteen years old I couldn't drive, so I depended on my sisters to give me rides to and from work. There were times that my sisters were late getting out of work, so Lucille would wait for me or give me rides home so I wouldn't be left alone waiting outside the fire department. I remember being in awe while riding in her luxury cars. I would share with Lucille that I wanted to pursue a career in science or health care. She would jokingly say that she pictured me as a scientist with my own chauffeur.

Lucille was not only my first boss, but she treated me as a young friend, and I saw her as a mentor. She taught me how to talk to people with respect, both on the phone and in person. She taught me how to organize and file records. She taught me the microfiche machine, using typewriters and computers. She taught me programs like Microsoft Word, how to write letters and resumes. She taught me how to use the copier, fax machine, and handle the switchboard when none of the secretaries were available. Lucille gave me confidence to learn new things and believed that I would perform my duties to the best of my ability.

Lucille also took time to introduce me to firefighters, EMTs, and 911 operators after hearing that I was interested in a career in science or health care. She knew that I didn't have any role models in my family for such a career, so she took me to departments located below where I worked so that I could observe how 911 operators were handling emergencies. I was so amazed at how calm the operators were while handling such traumatic situations. I was fascinated at how important their jobs were in saving the lives of so many people every day. After meeting these types of professionals over three summers working for Lucille, my interest in pursuing a career in health care continued to grow. Lucille is one of the reasons that I am a physician today.

Over the years, Lucille has been present to celebrate my accomplishments alongside my family members. She celebrated with me as if I were one of her own children. She and her late husband John were at my high school graduation. She attended my commencement at UC Irvine and celebrated with my family when I graduated medical school before I embarked on residency training in Missouri.

We continue to meet for a meal as often as possible whenever I visit my family in California. I will always be grateful to Lucille for investing time to teach me life skills and mentoring me to never forget those less fortunate than me.

Lucille has retired from the Orange County Fire Department. She is a devout practicing Catholic and participates in many ministries at the local church in Anaheim, California and she has volunteered at the cancer center at a hospital in Orange, California. Lucille is one reason I am inspired to find ways to give back to my community no matter how busy my schedule may be. Because of her strong faith, I think of her often as I find myself needing to defend my Catholic beliefs while practicing medicine in this secular society.

Villa Park High School

In 1987, my family moved to a new neighborhood in the city of Orange, which meant I had to attend a different high school than the one my older sisters had attended. It was hard to be separated from all my friends, whom I had known since elementary school. I attended Villa Park High School from 1988 to 1992, which was a major adjustment. There were only a handful of Vietnamese students in my class; I estimate that Villa Park High School had an Asian population of 30–40% at that time, but not the Vietnamese student population I was accustomed to at my previous schools. The students at Villa Park High School were also much more affluent compared to students at previous schools I had attended. I had feelings of inadequacy due to my family's low to middle-class status, which made it difficult for me to assimilate. I was socially timid, so I had to find a way to academically connect and succeed in this new environment.

During my freshman year at Villa Park High, I was given the opportunity to compete in the school science fair. I met with my chemistry professor, Dr. Steven Ebert, to discuss an experiment using citric acid to kill bacteria. He taught me how to grow *Bacillus subtilis* in an incubator, make various concentrations of citric acid, and expose the bacteria to citric acid. I showed that culture plates exposed to increasing amounts of citric acid had fewer bacteria growing, demonstrating the role of vitamin C (citric acid) in fighting bacterial infection, and I created a poster presentation for the school science fair. The only family member that showed up the night of my school science fair was my brother Huy, because he was the only sibling available to bring me to this

event. My parents rarely came to school events because they didn't speak English. Huy was there for moral support, but we were both shocked when my name was called to accept the Sweepstakes Trophy, the highest honor for the school science fair. I was featured on the front page of the school newspaper, and I went on to represent my school at the Orange County Science Fair later that year. Between the school science fair and the county science fair, my dad helped me improve my display from a three-panel

Science Fair Winner... Doan Nguyen, sweepstakes winner of the Villa Park Science Fair, experiments with Bacillus Subtilis in citric acid.

Doan Nguyen Takes First in Science Fair

by Jolleen Johnson

Doan Nguyen chose to try her luck with "The Effect of Citric Acid on Bacillus could have guessed the re- sult because the bacteria isn't near as strong as Vi- tamin C," commented Noo... found out the answers." Doan would like to go into the field of preventive medicine and she would

cardboard box to a three-panel styrofoam poster board. I think my parents began to see that my passion for science was real, and they tried to support me in any way they could, even though their knowledge of English and science was minimal.

During my senior year, I heard about the application for the school science medallions, only four of which were awarded to graduating seniors each year for excellence in science. I didn't think I stood a chance since the top contenders had parents who were physicians and pharmacists. My father was a fisherman and my mother worked at the grocery stores in the seafood department until her late forties. Who was I to think I had any chance to win a science medallion?

I was invited to an awards dinner towards the end of my senior year for students who had achieved at least a 4.0 grade point average. It was also the night when medallion winners for each department at Villa Park High School would be announced. My sister Pauline joined me for the dinner, which was held at the Orange County Mining Company, a beautiful restaurant perched at the top of Orange Hills. She drove a 1987 gray Toyota Corolla, which was eventually shared between the six sisters over eleven years. It was a car that had trouble starting in the winter and overheated in the summer. The battery died often, so it was no surprise to me when she pulled up to have the car valet parked (the only option for this restaurant), the car didn't start until the third try. It was all worth the embarrassment though, because at the end of the night, I not only walked away with a 4.0 plaque but also one of the four science medallions. What an honor! I will forever cherish that night when I made my family very proud.

Graduation day at Villa Park High School

2

An Education in Science

University of California, Irvine

I ATTENDED THE UNIVERSITY OF California, Irvine from September 1992 to June 1996, graduating with a Bachelor of Science degree in biological sciences. When I started college, I didn't yet know I wanted to pursue a career in medicine. I thought about pharmacy school and volunteered one summer with Drs. Robert and Nancy Ko at St. Joseph's Pharmacy, but after I shadowed these two pharmacists, I realized what I observed was not exciting enough for me.

I then decided to pursue volunteer opportunities at Western Medical Center in Santa Ana, California. I was placed in the emergency room for six months, which gave me a fast-paced view of medicine. Within the first month, I kept hearing phases like *code blue*, *time of death*, and *DOA*. It was surreal to see the other side of medicine, where not everyone can be saved despite all the knowledge and technology we have. I saw the sadness in the doctors' and nurses' eyes when they lost another patient. Some nights, I would drive home and think of the patients who died during my volunteer shift. I wasn't sure if I would be able to handle all the disappointments involved in this career path.

After six months in the emergency room, I decided that I wanted to volunteer in the neonatal intensive care unit, which I thought might give me a slower-paced view of medicine and a focus on children. I ended up spending four hours almost every weekend there for about two years. It was wonderful to witness the amazing work of the neonatologists, pediatric specialists, and surgeons who saved these babies' lives. I learned about Hirschsprung's disease (a condition in which a baby is born without nerve cells in parts of the large intestine, preventing it from functioning properly) for the first time when a baby from Russia was brought to Western Medical Center for treatment. Following successful surgeries for Hirschsprung's disease, at around four months of age he was feeding by mouth and having normal bowel movements, so he was able to return to Russia. I also saw an anencephalic baby—born with an underdeveloped brain and an incomplete skull—who was being monitored until his Catholic parents made the decision to withdraw care. His monitors would constantly alarm because of his erratic heart rate and breathing pattern. Again, I saw the joy of providing life-saving treatment and the disappointment of not having much to offer to a patient.

I was awarded an Auxiliary Volunteer scholarship from Western Medical Center while studying at UC Irvine. It was an honor to have Lucille Mello from the Orange County Fire Department and my research mentor, Dr. Edward Arquilla, attend the awards ceremony. This was a turning point in my career because I realized that other people in the healthcare field saw my passion to care for patients and wanted to encourage me to pursue this career path.

Receiving the Auxiliary Volunteer scholarship

Edward R. Arquilla, MD, PhD

I first met Dr. Arquilla when I signed up for a research elective during my junior year at UC Irvine. I was still trying to decide if I wanted to apply for medical school or graduate school. His advice guiding me towards a career in healthcare rather than research really solidified my decision to pursue medical school, perhaps much later in college than most of my peers. My grades were above average and my research experience made me competitive, or so I thought. I prepared for and took the Medical College Admission Test (MCAT) several times, but my scores were not strong enough to compete with applicants to medical schools in the United States. However, I was determined that if it was meant to be then God would guide me to the opportunity to pursue this career. In the meantime, I continued to work with Dr. Arquilla on various research projects and presented at the UCI Campuswide Research Symposium.

I am forever grateful to Dr. Arquilla for mentoring me to pursue a career in medicine, although my path to get there was more tortuous than his. He told me that patients don't really care that much where a physician went to medical school as long as the physician is well trained, dedicated, and compassionate towards them.

The last time I spoke to Dr. Arquilla was during my medical residency. I had lunch with him during one of my trips back to California sometime between 2002 and 2006. He talked about me coming back to do research with him when I completed my medical training. He was one of the earliest influences in my career, and I will forever be grateful that he offered me the opportunity to work with him in research and to appreciate the challenges of academic medicine.

I recall how Dr. Arquilla would always end his days at the office by telling me, "Take care." This is something I still say to my patients these days when ending my interactions with them, and each time I utter those words to them, I remember Dr. Arquilla.

During my junior year at UC Irvine, I decided to pursue research opportunities to build my resume. I took a research course with Dr. Arquilla in the Department of Pathology. I learned how to perform radio-immune assays to measure insulin and insulin-antibody levels in maternal and cord blood, and I learned the ELISA (enzyme-linked immunosorbent assay) method to measure specific insulin antibodies. We were trying to determine whether a fetus had its own immune system or if its immune system was determined only by the passage of antibodies from the mother to the fetus through the placenta. I learned to analyze data and in the process acquired many computer skills that continue to help me in my career.

By the end of my junior year at UC Irvine, I had solidified my decision to pursue a career in medicine. I realized that God had given me a talent to listen to people and an innate compassion for those less fortunate than me. I felt a calling to use that talent no matter how difficult my path to medicine might be. I had taken the MCATs many times but had only average scores, not competitive enough to be accepted to American medical schools. I was accepted to the UC Irvine Post-Baccalaureate Program, which helped minority students enter professional school. I again excelled in advanced courses in biochemistry, molecular biology, and physiology, but when it came to the MCATs, I was still unable to improve my scores.

Just when I thought my hopes to pursue a medical career were gone, something amazing happened. I was walking along one of the hallways at UCI reading things posted on bulletin boards. I suddenly saw a flyer with information about the American University of the Caribbean School of Medicine. I was curious and researched the school, and I discovered that this medical school required MCAT scores but did not place great emphasis on them as part of the admission decision. I also learned from a few people at UCI that they knew people who had graduated from this medical school and were able to get a medical residency in the United States. I prayed about this decision, then prepared my documents to apply for admission. It took several months before I finally heard about my application, but finally I was accepted to the American University of the Caribbean School of Medicine to matriculate in August 1998. That was among one of the best days of my life.

Graduation day at UC Irvine

3

Embarking on a Medical Career

AMERICAN UNIVERSITY OF THE CARIBBEAN
SCHOOL OF MEDICINE

The Basic Science Experience

WHEN PEOPLE LEARN THAT I attended medical school in the Caribbean, the immediate question is "How hard could medical school have been?" People seem to have a stereotyped impression that our classes were held on the beach and that students spent more time sunbathing than doing dissections in anatomy lab. To dispel the myths about the journey of a Caribbean medical student, I want to share my experiences living in St. Maarten for the first twenty months of medical school.

There are three matriculating classes each year at the American University of the Caribbean (AUC) School of Medicine, each entering in January, May, or August. The basic science curriculum is completed in twenty months, divided into five semesters. There is at most a two-week break between semesters, so many students do not fly home at the end of every semester. For this reason, we often missed out on holidays and vacations with our families. Even when we wanted to escape the island after long weeks of studying for exams, we often couldn't do this because of financial

My first visit to St. Maarten before deciding to attend AUC

constraints. The cost of living on an island was much higher. The basic necessities that people in the United States take for granted such as water and toilet paper were overpriced for tourists. To stay within a reasonable budget, two to three students usually shared one-bedroom apartments and took turns sleeping on the couch or the floor. We not only split rent and utilities but also shared the cost of groceries to make ends meet. We shared responsibilities of getting or making dinner, taking into account which roommates were having exams that week.

In 1998 during my first semester, Hurricane George made landfall on St. Maarten as a category 3 storm. Between the storm and difficulties in getting student loans, nearly half of students enrolled that semester dropped out. In the fall of 1999, Hurricane Jose (category 2) and Hurricane Lenny (category 5) made landfall. Natural disasters often adversely affected our curriculum schedule. Classes were cancelled for a few days, but then when school resumed, class hours doubled the week after hurricanes in order to keep exams on schedule. I remember one classmate knocked on the door of the pathology professor in the middle of one hurricane to ask if the midterm exam was being postponed. He said he would double up on lectures to help us get ready for the exam.

During hurricanes, many of us studied in our homes by candlelight or using bat- tery-operated lanterns in our homes. The school itself was built to withstand a category 5 hurricane and had its own generator. Sometimes we would wait until the calm of the eye of the storm to make a quick trip to school to study. We brought our sleeping bags and pillows and camped out in the library in between bookshelves and tables. We also were able to take advantage of the school's internet service to send an email to our families back home and let them know that we were safe.

Class picture after completing second year of medical school in St. Maarten. This was the last photo together before we all went on to clinical rotations.

As you can see, life's not a beach for a medical student in St. Maarten. The challenge was to avoid the beach in order to be successful during the basic science curriculum months, and it was tempting to be a tourist instead of a student. I had to learn that there were only a few days each semester where it was okay to be a tourist and enjoy the beauty that the island had to offer.

My time in medical school was the most desolate time in my life. I felt alone in my decision to pursue medicine and to move to a Caribbean island. The only connection I had with my family was through God. It was the first time in my life that I could choose to practice my religion or not. With all the values entrenched in me during my childhood experiences, I felt that my life would not be complete without God. I practiced an abbreviated version of Catholic rituals, but I still did it every day. I said prayers before I went to class and always before bedtime. I prayed to God personally for help, enlightenment, inspiration, guidance, strength, and willpower to fight temptations. I asked God to tell me what He had in store for me. I thanked God for keeping me safe every day. I learned to turn any struggle into a positive experience. With struggles, I asked for God's help to endure them. My relationship with God strengthened and it became one of love, not fear. What I had gotten out of catechism classes was that I was to avoid sin or else God would punish me. I lived the early part of my life constantly concerned about whether I had offended God and whether I was digging my hole to hell. This was the beginning of a change in my view of religion and spirituality.

I went through Category 3, 4, and 5 hurricanes during my 20-month basic science curriculum in St. Maarten. I developed a strong camaraderie with my roommates and classmates because of the hardships we went through together. We shared water, food, electricity, and love for one another, but most of all, we shared our commitment to succeed. These experiences helped strengthen our resolve to become physicians so that we could help the less fortunate people in our communities. Many Caribbean medical school graduates have a drive to succeed and to help the less fortunate, especially because we've been through difficult times ourselves. During those hurricanes, I remember the satisfaction of knowing that my rice cooker, dried pork, and instant noodles helped feed many people in my class. We bonded in a special way because each of us truly cared about one another. Any sense of competitiveness amongst medical school classmates was minimized and we were reminded of why we wanted to pursue careers in medicine in the first place. After surviving the hurricanes and graduating from medical school, I saw that God again had given me a second chance.

Clinical Clerkships

Medical students are required to do core rotations during their third year, which includes internal medicine, surgery, pediatrics, obstetrics/gynecology, and psychiatry. At some schools, family medicine was also a required core rotation. During their fourth year, students were allowed to choose elective rotations, which gave them an opportunity to focus more on areas of interest that would help them develop their future careers. For instance, I did more fourth-year rotations related to pediatrics and internal medicine because a combination of internal medicine and pediatrics was going to be my residency of choice.

Internal medicine was my first clinical rotation, and I started at St. Agnes Hospital in Baltimore, Maryland. It was a twelve-week rotation where I learned to start my day around 6:00 a.m. and accept that my day would end when my chief resident excused me to go home, which was typically after 6:00 p.m. I had to get comfortable with gathering patient data quickly and presenting the information in a comprehensive way during rounds. I was always nervous about whether I pronounced words correctly or even understood what I was saying at all. The very first patient I interviewed and presented for morning rounds was an African-American nurse who had a goiter due to thyroid condition called Graves' disease. It was hard to concentrate on taking a history when all I wanted to do was to examine the goiter and read all about Graves' disease. That was the challenge in medical school—balancing my studies with hands-on experience. Sometimes we read things and thought we knew it well until we were asked about it on rounds and realized we missed the big picture or a critical piece of information. Regardless, when we missed something on rounds, we never forgot it again. I continued to build on my knowledge during my internal medicine rotation, which helped me with my first PowerPoint case presentation at the end of the rotation, a literature discussion on the relationship between pancreatitis, hypertriglyceridemia, and diabetes. I was awarded the best student presentation for that rotation.

After internal medicine, I had to compete for a spot to do my twelve-week surgical rotation at St. Agnes Hospital. I was glad to know that the residents and attending physicians I encountered during my internal medicine rotation were supportive of my application for the surgical rotation. I spent four weeks on vascular surgery and eight weeks on general surgery. These were the most grueling months of my medical school experience, not least because it happened during the winter months and I experienced driving in snowy weather for the first time. Somehow, I survived the weather and my sleepless nights during surgery clerkship.

After I completed my surgery rotation, I was assigned to psychiatry rotation at the Metropolitan State Hospital in Norwalk, California, which was less than one hour away from my parents' home in Orange. It was a nice reprieve to be near family after being away from home for almost two years. I was pampered with Vietnamese food and blessed with wonderful family gatherings. I didn't take this opportunity for granted since I didn't know if I would see my family much after this rotation. So almost every weekend for six weeks, I went home to spend time with my parents, siblings, nieces, and nephews.

Psychiatry rotation was quite a shift after rotating through internal medicine and surgery. Students were responsible for guarding their badges used to enter the hospital gates. We were also responsible for the keys to enter the building and the patient units. Security had to be alerted and the unit went on lockdown if students lost their keys or badge. We had few, if any, opportunities to do one-on-one interviews with patients. Rounds were done as a group, each of us taking turns asking the patient a series of questions while the patient sat at the head of a table. Our attending physician would prompt us when it was our turn to come up with a question that would help determine the diagnosis and treatment plan for the patient.

I remember a few times during morning rounds when I wondered if the stories told by the psychiatry patients were true. One patient said that he was admitted to Metropolitan State Hospital because he tried to kill his brother, whom he thought had inherited a poinsettia farm. He told the team interviewing him that his grandfather had invented poinsettias. Another patient claimed that President George H. W. Bush asked him to save the ozone layer by flying a plane and spraying ozone to plug up the holes in the sky. After a few weeks on psychiatry, we gradually learned that it was much more challenging to get a reliable history from psychiatry patients.

After psychiatry, I spent the next sixteen weeks in Brooklyn, New York at Wyckoff Heights Medical Center doing pediatric and obstetrics/gynecology rotations. I was looking forward to pediatrics because I have always enjoyed working with children. I was so proud to become an aunt when I was fourteen years old, and I just loved babysitting my nieces and nephews. I excelled in pediatrics, and it solidified my commitment to pursuing a career involving children. As for OB/GYN, I had mixed feelings about the joy of bringing a new life into the world while at the same time seeing women terminate their pregnancies. I was asked to assist in termination of pregnancies, but once I found out what I was suctioning during the procedures, I requested to not be assigned to these procedures. Once, I assisted in the delivery of a stillborn baby at thirty-two weeks from a woman who claimed she did not know she was ever pregnant. I believe this was a juncture in my training at which I struggled with ethics in medicine and how my Catholic faith would shape my medical career.

One of the hot topics in American politics is abortion, and it will likely continue to be an issue that defines the moral fabric of the United States. I am an active member of the Catholic Medical Association and my Facebook profile describes me as a "Vietnamese-American Pro-Life Catholic physician." If a nation like ours believes that we are "one nation under God," then we must believe God governs all aspects of our lives. I believe that God gives life and God determines when life ends. In the medical profession, I have witnessed many times when people who were thought not to have any chance of survival ended up walking out of the hospital a few weeks after admission. I have also seen people going to renowned institutions to get the best physicians who end up dying within days of getting the "best treatment." There are many parents who are told their babies would never grow up to be "normal" or they should consider abortion because of a genetic condition not compatible with normal development. Many of these parents will later tell stories of how their decision not to terminate their pregnancy allowed them to witness God's purpose for bringing that child into this world. I believe that Divine intervention is the reason for things that happen but cannot be explained by modern science.

I pray that God will once again reign strong in American society. I pray for religious leaders and politicians to defend life from conception to natural death. If people are punished for harming animals, why is killing a human being in the womb not considered murder? When a pregnant woman is murdered, the suspect is charged with two murders. So why is killing of a baby in the womb not a crime? If a physician ends a code and declares "time of death" when a person's heart stops, then why do we not consider the beginning of life when there is evidence of a heartbeat? I ask you to consider these questions for yourself and not allow the media or politicians to tell you how to think. My upbringing in the conservative Vietnamese culture and the Catholic faith has made me an unwavering defender of life. I am honored to say that on October 6, 2019, I participated in a pro-life prayer service at Holy Family Catholic Church to pray for the end to abortion. I was also able to attend the March for Life in Chicago on January 11, 2020, for the first time in my life.

After my third-year rotations were completed and while I was preparing for my United States Medical Licensing Examination (USMLE) Step 2 exam, the tragedy of September 11, 2001, happened. After finishing my OB/GYN rotation in July 2001 in New York, I thought about staying there to take a board review course in Manhattan with my friends. For some reason, I decided to go back to Baltimore instead of staying in New York. My friends who remained in New York became part of the healthcare team serving the overwhelming number of patients who needed emergency care and surgeries due to the injuries from the 9/11 attack on the World Trade Center. I returned to New York in November 2001 to interview for residency, and I remember the overwhelming sadness I felt witnessing the devastation of the attack on this country.

During my fourth year of medical school, I did electives at St. Agnes Hospital in Baltimore; Aultman Hospital in Canton, Ohio; MetroHealth Medical Center in Cleveland, Ohio; and the University of Missouri-Columbia. The opportunity to live in so many places throughout the United States helped me determine what type of living environment suited me best. I realized that I didn't like the big city life, but wanted to live in a smaller city that was near a big city. As my career progressed, I searched for jobs that fit this criteria. I also wanted relatively low cost of living and minimal traffic so I could get to and from work within twenty or thirty minutes. I felt that all cities have some crime, so there was no avoiding that factor, especially when I usually wanted to live somewhat close to the hospitals where I was employed.

The first time that I really felt homesick was Christmas of 2001 while living in Canton. I was staying at a family-owned extended stay motel that charged me a monthly rate. It had a microwave, a small refrigerator, and a toaster in the shared kitchenette. I leased a car and the locals taught me how to defrost my car and scrape snow and ice from my windshield. Because I was staying there during the winter holiday season but didn't have family nearby, I watched the Food Network channel to feel warm and fuzzy inside. I missed a first cousin's wedding that most of my family members were attending that December. Over time, I began to realize that I was going to miss a lot of holidays and family events, so I might as well get used to it. I didn't want to cry about it or let anyone feel sorry for me, so I kept phone calls to my family very brief. When I did call, I let my family know that I was fine, and I updated them on my new address each time I started a new clinical rotation in a different city.

Living in Cleveland was quite a memorable experience. I was doing clinical rotations there in February and March 2002, so I experienced lake-effect snow. It would take me at least forty-five minutes to drive three or four miles, and I couldn't see the other side of the street because of all the snow piled up on either side of the road. This was one reason why I turned down an offer to sign outside the National Residency Matching Program (known as the Match) for a family practice residency position at MetroHealth Medical Center. The other reason was safety concerns while living there. It was soon after 9/11 when I began traveling outside of Baltimore for other electives. I was scheduled to fly from Baltimore to Cleveland and then planned to drive to Canton for my pediatric sub-internship and NICU rotation at Aultman Hospital. I had set up electives at MetroHealth Medical Center for February and March, but I didn't have a place to stay yet. Before boarding the flight, another gentleman and I were pulled out of the boarding line for a random search. I had my tweezers and nail clippers confiscated from my toiletries bag but was allowed to board. I ended up sitting next to that gentleman, who turned out to be a real estate agent in Cleveland. We started chatting about our being randomly searched before boarding and then he asked me what brought me to Cleveland. I told him I was a medical student and was looking for a place in Cleveland to stay during February and March. To my surprise, he had a three-bedroom unfurnished apartment on the west side for $500 a month. As a medical student on student loans, that sounded like a wonderful deal and I felt like God was looking down on me. We exchanged phone numbers and the next day I signed the lease.

Needless to say, it was too good to be true. After I moved in, I found out that the street I lived on was formerly known for drug dealers and sex workers. My neighbors downstairs would slam the door and yell at each other almost every night. I could hardly sleep, worried that any night there would be shots fired through my floor or that someone might break into my home by mistake; I later found out that my neighbors were using and dealing drugs. I still look back on my naiveté and wonder if I would have signed the same lease for that apartment today. Desperate situations call for desperate measures, but at least I had a place to live for my clinical rotations at MetroHealth Medical Center. I didn't have time to think about it or talk it over with my family. I felt that I had to take it while it was available or risk not having a place to live at all.

The first time in my life I ever called 911 for a police escort was to walk me to my apartment at night in Cleveland. I travelled to California one weekend to meet with my mom's cardiologist to discuss her heart failure and coronary artery disease. When I came back from the airport after a delayed flight, it was too dark and scary to walk up to my apartment alone, so I called the police for an escort. I was informed by the officers that the people congregating outside my apartment and blocking the entrance to my front door were drug users and dealers, and they were well known to the police department. Making split-second decisions like calling for a police escort was what helped me survive Cleveland.

After Cleveland, I was so excited to move to Columbia, Missouri for my last rotation in medical school. I had signed outside the Match with the University of Missouri–Columbia (Mizzou) to be an internal medicine-pediatrics resident from 2002 to 2006. I remember calling my mom on the plane ride back from interviewing at Mizzou, where the school mascot was a tiger, and telling her I'd decided to do my residency there. I was a Tiger by Chinese Zodiac sign, and now I was going to be a Mizzou Tiger resident. I saw this sign as a fascinating coincidence that I was meant to spend part of my training in Columbia, Missouri.

Medical school graduation in St. Maarten, June 2002

4

A Tiger Joins the Tigers

In July 2002, I started my internal medicine-pediatrics residency at the University of Missouri–Columbia, and I purchased my first house. At the time, banks had a deal for physicians which allowed me to buy a house without a down payment as long as I had enough credit and income to show I could pay the mortgage. I didn't have my own car, so my family shipped an older car to Missouri for me to use during training. Until the car arrived, I leased a car just like I had done throughout my medical school rotations.

I learned so much about being a homeowner. I couldn't just call the landlord when something was broken, and I had to find out who was trustworthy for many services I needed. During the first month of residency I was assigned to the pediatric floor, and I left my house before sunrise and returned after sunset. By the end of July, I received a letter from the fire department telling me that my backyard was a fire hazard. That was when I finally looked outside to see that my seeded backyard had grown into a jungle of yellow, dried grass. I was so stressed and didn't know what to do. That's when I talked to my neighbor, Bob Hathman, who used his John Deere riding mower to plow down the backyard. Thanks to Bob, I also picked out a lawn mower at Lowe's, learned how to fill the lawn mower with oil and gas, and how to start it to mow my own yard. It would take a few tries to start the mower, and I would hear some chuckles from my neighbors.

When I faced my first major snowstorm in Missouri, I realized that my driveway was on an incline and it was impossible to drive into the garage when there was ice and snow on the driveway. A Cambodian man across the street saw that I was revving my car without success, slipping and sliding off the driveway. He came over with his snowblower and chipped away the ice so I could get into my garage.

I always felt so indebted to my neighbors for their kindness. I prayed for them and also found ways to show my gratitude, such as bringing them baked goods or cutting them a bouquet of tulips from my garden. I felt like God had put these people in my life to serve as my guardian angels.

Alejandro Ramirez, MD

When I was a resident at the University of Missouri–Columbia from 2002 to 2006, I had the opportunity to work with Dr. Ramirez. He is by far the kindest physician I have ever met. I don't recall ever seeing him get mad about anything or at anybody. That didn't mean he didn't teach students and residents effectively; he just taught in a non-threatening, nurturing way.

I knew after my first year of residency that I wanted to pursue a second half-day each week seeing patients in the pediatric gastroenterology clinic with Dr. Ramirez. I would ask to observe and assist with procedures he performed and help with inpatient consultations if I had free time while on other elective rotations or if he needed help. I knew very early in my residency that I would one day want to apply for a pediatric gastroenterology fellowship. I wanted to soak up as much knowledge and experience as possible so that I would be prepared for fellowship application. All of these extra things I did to build my curriculum vitae were made possible with the dedicated mentorship of Dr. Ramirez.

I am forever grateful to Dr. Ramirez for reminding me to be a kind, compassionate physician and for inspiring me to pursue a career in pediatric gastroenterology. Without his training, mentorship, and support of my fellowship application, I would not be where I am today.

During my third year at Mizzou, I applied for and was awarded a CATCH (Community Access To Child Health) grant from the American Academy of Pediatrics for a proposal to increase access to health care for uninsured and underserved populations in Columbia. Together with other residents, I was able to offer free health screenings, connect children with primary care physicians, and get children signed up for government-subsidized health insurance programs like Medicaid or CHIP if their families qualified. At the time, I didn't know how much of an impact this grant would have on the rest of my career. It helped me recognize my desire for community service and my ability to bring together people of different talents to make a difference in the lives of those less fortunate than me.

> *Being awarded a CATCH grant helped me recognize my desire for community service and my ability to bring together people of different talents to make a difference in the lives of those less fortunate than me.*

While in residency training at Mizzou, I experienced the challenges of training for a career in medicine while trying to figure out my personal life. While I was in undergraduate college at UC Irvine, I met my first boyfriend, whom I dated for about seven years. He was a wonderful person, but for various reasons the timing wasn't right. I was too ambitious to settle down in my twenties, and I was still trying to figure out where my medical training was headed, so I broke off the relationship while I was in medical school in St. Maarten. It was painful, but deep in my heart I knew we were going separate ways in our personal and professional journeys.

After I broke up with my college boyfriend, I dated a medical student who was a few semesters behind me. I thought we had things in common such as being Vietnamese and Catholic, and pursuing a career in medicine. As we continued to see each other and after I met his family, I gradually realized that we were more different than I had thought. I considered myself conservative, but he was ultra-conservative and still held very traditional Vietnamese cultural views such as male dominance in a relationship. Sometimes I felt like I was just a trophy he was showing off to his family and friends. But when his family and friends were not around, he was very controlling and became jealous if I talked to other male medical students. He didn't even want me to help any students but him.

Because I felt like we were not seeing eye-to-eye about our relationship and I felt trapped by his controlling personality, I told him I wanted to end the relationship in spring 2002 before I started my residency. After I broke off the relationship, I experienced a lot of anxiety about how he was going to handle the breakup. I was hoping that since we were both focusing on our medical careers, the break up would be civil and we could remain friends. I had such a bad experience with his controlling nature and jealousy issues that I just wanted to focus on starting my residency rather than having a social life at all.

He never told his parents that we broke up and he made them think everything was still great between us. I started residency in July 2002 at Mizzou and the stalking phone calls began. Either he or his friends would call my cell phone and say mean things on the phone to me. He even impersonated a police officer. I spoke to the Columbia Police Department one night because I was getting threatening messages. I hadn't given him or any of his friends the address to my new home. He called up my brother-in-law in Boston, who didn't know we had broken up, so my brother-in-law gave him my new address.

One day in early January 2003, I was in my backyard and my garage was open. All of a sudden I saw a car parked outside my house and a guy walking up to it. I locked the door from the garage to my house and ran inside to call 911. The guy was pounding on the door to my garage. I quickly turned my attention to the sliding glass door to my backyard and tried to pull it shut just as the guy—who had run around the back of the house at this point—grabbed hold of it. I screamed on the phone to the 911 operator for help and then ran to the front door. Just then, a police officer pulled up to the front of my house, ran into the house and arrested the intruder. It turned out to be my ex-boyfriend from medical school.

Luckily, I had filed an order of protection against my ex-boyfriend prior to this incident due to his threatening phone calls and messages, so I handed the papers to the police officer. My ex ended up in jail overnight and was bailed out. Following the attempted break-in, he was scheduled to appear for a hearing at the Columbia Municipal Court, where I applied for the order of protection to be extended for one year. The extension was granted due to him not showing up. I agreed to have the felony charge dropped to a misdemeanor so as not to ruin his opportunity for a medical career. To this day, I don't know if he ever finished medical school. Needless to say, it was a tumultuous time in my life and I remained very guarded for a while when dealing with my single male co-workers at the hospital.

Columbia will always be dear to my heart because it is where I met my husband, Marconi, during my first year of residency. After trying multiple times to strike up conversations with me between July 2002 and January 2003, he finally asked me out. It seemed like we were meant to meet. Even though he was doing his preliminary year in general surgery, he was usually assigned to do consults wherever I worked. In late January 2003, he had finished doing otolaryngology (ear, nose, and throat) consults and called me to say he had cleared my patients to be discharged. When I told him I already discharged those patients, he proceeded to ask if I was free that weekend—clearly Marconi was using this encounter as an excuse to ask me out. I have to admit that I was hesitant to date anyone after having to deal with my ex's stalking behavior, so at first I tried to find ways out of this situation. I told him I was on call that Friday night and post-call (a time period residents use to rest up for their next on-call shift) on Saturday. When Marconi asked me for my number, I told him he already had my pager number. In the end, he decided to give me his number in case I wanted to go to dinner. Eventually I relented and we went out to dinner on January 25, which happened to be my dad's birthday.

After our first year together at Mizzou, Marconi changed to family medicine residency and transferred to Southern Illinois University in Springfield. I still had to finish my residency in Columbia, so for about three years we had a long-distance relationship. Marconi told me that if we were still together at the end of our residencies, we would get married. I suppose that was his proposal three years ahead of time.

In 2004, during my third year of residency, I started applying for a pediatric gastroenterology fellowship. It is a very competitive fellowship, and most programs offer only two paid fellowship positions per year. Being a foreign medical graduate, I felt like I was already at a disadvantage. However, I trusted in certain accomplishments such as being a recipient of the American Academy of Pediatrics CATCH grant as a distinguishing aspect of my curriculum vitae. I remember receiving rejection letters, going through interviews and not being offered a position. The search for a fellowship position continued into my fourth year. By the middle of that year, I had interviewed at the University of Iowa and the University of Florida. Around December 2005, I interviewed at SUNY Downstate Medical Center in Brooklyn, New York, on the last day for interviews for that program. I met Dr. William Treem, who was the fellowship program director. I was among four or five candidates interviewing that day, but I felt quite confident when I left. I remember Dr. Treem asking me to tell him why he should hire me over all the other candidates. It was the first time in my life when I had to brag about myself, something I'm not used to doing.

About a month later, I was driving back from the airport in St. Louis after Marconi and I had been on vacation. I received a phone call from Dr. Treem, who offered me the one available position for a pediatric gastroenterology fellowship to start July 2006. I had two weeks to make a decision. I still had invitations to interview at Northwestern University in Evanston, Illinois, and Johns Hopkins University in Baltimore. On the other hand, Marconi's relatives lived in the New York metropolitan area. He really hoped that I would get a fellowship position in New York

William R. Treem, MD

Pediatric gastroenterology fellowship is one of the most competitive training programs in medicine. I began my fellowship applications during my third year of residency but did not get an offer until the middle of my fourth and final year. To say that there was so much uncertainty in my career at that point would be an understatement.

While Marconi and I were dating, he told me that he hoped I would get accepted to a pediatric GI fellowship in the New York area because he had lots of relatives there. I told him that based on my first round of applications, all the positions in New York were already filled. However, to my surprise there was an unexpected opening for a first year fellowship position at SUNY Downstate Medical Center in Brooklyn, New York. Apparently the physician that had accepted the position during the first round had decided to withdraw his acceptance.

Dr. Treem was the pediatric gastroenterology fellowship program director at SUNY Downstate. Dr. Ramirez, who was mentoring me during residency, was a member of the North American Society of Pediatric Gastroenterology, Hepatology and Nutrition (NASPGHAN). He had seen an email within the Pediatric GI Bulletin Board courtesy of NASPGHAN where program directors were asking for applications to fill fellowship vacancies. Once I heard about the SUNY Downstate position from Dr. Ramirez, I applied after speaking to Dr. Treem over the phone. I interviewed in person in December 2015 and later learned that Dr. Treem spent the most time with me out of all the candidates who interviewed that day. I also learned that I was competing with close to sixty applicants for the one fellowship position. About one month after the interview, Dr. Treem offered me the position, which I decided to accept.

I will forever be grateful to Dr. Treem for seeing my strength as a compassionate person who wanted to serve the poor, needy, and underserved. He recognized that I would stand up for what is right to ensure patient safety and quality of care, and he trusted that I would speak up to make sure all trainees were being treated fairly and not mistreated by their superiors; he later supported me through struggles I had with my research mentor after I made him aware of the situation. During my training, he inspired me to recognize interesting cases to write up for publication as a way to develop my clinical research skills. He also guided me to develop a laboratory project that led to my first basic science research publication in the Journal of Pediatric Gastroenterology and Nutrition. He realized that I didn't have the most helpful research mentor, but I always tried to make the best of any situation. He told me that wherever I go after fellowship training, I have the personality to persevere in any environment. Most of all, I am very blessed to have Dr. Treem as a lifelong mentor in my professional development, one who cares about my personal well-being as I continue to practice medicine in an environment that has become more business-driven than quality-focused.

and here was the offer. But do I take this and not ever know if I had a chance to be accepted at the remaining programs? During the next two weeks, I decided to call Northwestern and Johns Hopkins to decline their offers to interview, and finally I contacted Dr. Treem to accept the fellowship position. That was the best decision I have ever made in my entire medical career.

Marconi and I got engaged on a cruise to Ensenada, Mexico in 2005.

One of my favorite movies is *Father of the Bride*. It was the movie I watched alone the night that I made the decision to inform my family that I would be getting married to Marconi—he had finally proposed in March 2005 while we were on a cruise to Ensenada, Mexico. It was among the most difficult conversations I have ever had with my family in my adult life. In retrospect, I think my family was apprehensive about my marriage because nobody in my family had ever married outside of our faith or culture. To make matters more difficult, Marconi and I had chosen to marry in Missouri instead of California—Vietnamese tradition calls for weddings to be in the bride's hometown—and we would be forgoing the traditional Vietnamese ceremonies that take place on the morning of a wedding. I tried talking to my parents and brothers by telephone, then wrote them a letter, then eventually flew with Marconi to California to set the record straight. I was faced with the choice of delaying my wedding plans to a date deemed more acceptable to my family or keeping my wedding date on June 17, 2006, and risk not having anyone in my family attend. It was very painful to be going through this process in my head all alone at my house in Columbia. I remember thinking: Why couldn't my family just accept my decision and be happy for me? I thought I was supposed to be Daddy's little girl. My sisters Huong and Hong tried to talk to my family to smooth things out and I was very appreciative of their efforts.

I would talk to Marconi, his parents, and his cousins, who couldn't understand why my family wasn't happy that I found my lifetime partner. I was also faced with the fear of losing Marconi, who felt like my family was never going to accept him because he was neither Catholic nor Vietnamese. I remember crying alone every time I came home from a long day at work during my residency. I prayed to God for guidance and for God to enlighten my family to get past any biases they might have against Marconi.

Before the wedding, Marconi and I met many times with Father Phil Niekamp for guidance, support, and enlightenment. Father Phil would always say that if it was meant to be, everything would work out and my family would eventually come around. Father Phil was right, and my family did eventually embrace my decision. Marconi and I got married on June 17, 2006—Father's Day weekend—at Our Lady of Lourdes Catholic Church in Columbia with Father Phil and my two priest brothers presiding. It was also four days after I graduated from internal medicine residency and one day after my pediatric residency graduation. So much was happening in one week! Even though I was trying to hold in tears of sadness as I completed my residency, I also had tears of joy as I married Marconi in front of my family.

5

Pediatric Gastroenterology Fellowship

SUNY DOWNSTATE MEDICAL CENTER

AFTER OUR WEDDING, I HAD two weeks to move to New York and start my pediatric gastroenterology fellowship at SUNY Downstate Medical Center in New York. My mother-in-law and father-in-law got Marconi and I packed up from our homes in Missouri and Illinois for a long drive with a U-Haul to New York City. After we got there, we stayed at Marconi's aunt's house until we found an apartment in Brooklyn about one week later.

Finding an apartment in New York was harder than buying my house in Missouri. We paid about $1,700 per month for a 450-square-foot apartment in Fort Greene, compared to a mortgage payment of less than $1,000 per month for my 1,600-square-foot ranch-style home in Columbia, which also included a 2-car garage and a huge backyard with a covered patio. Downsizing our living space so much while paying a great deal more was quite a culture shock, so we learned to give away things and be grateful just to find a place we could afford.

It was not easy during that first year of our marriage. There were times I thought I had made a mistake getting married to Marconi but was too ashamed to admit it. Every time we argued, I prayed that God would help us work things out. I would let difficult times pass by shifting my focus from our marriage to my fellowship goals. Concentrating on patient care and research goals became a way out of stressing about the state of our marriage.

It has been said that financial issues are among the top reasons that marriages fail. I did not want that to be the story of our marriage, so I worked very hard to save money in any way I could. I would try to get by without having things but felt the need to splurge on clothes at Ann Taylor when I had my four days off each month during my first year of fellowship.

When I started my fellowship in July, I was paying for utilities, groceries, student loans, credit cards, rent, and the mortgage on my house in Missouri, which was not sold until September. Marconi did not have a license to practice medicine in New York until August, then he eventually found a job at the New York Hotel Trades Council in Harlem as a family physician working mostly in urgent care. At the time, I had too much pride to ask anyone for financial help. I applied for forbearance on my student loans from medical school just to keep my checking accounts in the black. At one point, I took out another credit card to pay for my mortgage until Marconi could get his first paycheck. I was upset at Marconi for not applying for his New York license while we were in Missouri so that he would be able to start a job and help me out while I was starting fellowship. I was the organized person who planned out every venture ahead of time, while he was the one always one step behind, and I just felt that he was selfish and not thoughtful.

I was so sad about how I felt in my marriage, and at the same time I was struggling with the busy schedule and loads of responsibilities as a first-year pediatric gastro-enterology fellow. I was sleep-deprived and under constant pressure to impress all my attending physicians. On the totem pole of medical training, I had just gone from the top as a graduating resident to the bottom as a first-year fellow. I felt disillusioned about my marriage and my career choices. I was afraid to call my family to share my pain and sadness because I didn't want to hear them say, "We told you so."

After my house sold in September, things got better. I was settling into fellowship and set on my next topic of discussion with Marconi about having kids. This raised the question: if we had kids, in what faith would they be raised? Marconi knew that my Catholic faith was very important to me and I would never give it up. I said that I would think about having kids with him if and only if he would convert to Catholicism. I was relieved when he agreed to go through the Rite of Christian Initiation of Adults (RCIA). I prayed a lot for him and attended a few of his RCIA classes when I was not on call. I wanted to show support and reinforce how important his decision to join the Catholic Church was to me. He was confirmed into the Catholic Church on April 7, 2007, during Easter Vigil Mass at Queen of All Saints Roman Catholic Church in Brooklyn. I am happy to say that he is a practicing Catholic. His family members are Christians and usually attend Episcopalian or non-denominational services. When we visit them, we go to Catholic Mass then attend their church services when invited to do so. I try to be open-minded about religion, but I will not abandon the practice of my

Catholic faith.

One of my goals during my fellowship was to be published in a reputable medical journal. At first, I was just excited to be a co-author on a paper, but then I had to raise the bar for myself—I wanted to be a lead author. By the second year of fellowship, my first case report was published in the February 2010 issue of *Journal of Pediatric Gastroenterology and Nutrition*, entitled "Oropharyngeal and Proximal Esophageal Involvement During Adalimumab Treatment of Crohn's Disease." I am grateful to Dr. Steven Schwarz, who mentored me in the completion of this manuscript. He gave me the confidence to tell my patient's story and justify to reviewers that my clinical research work was a significant contribution to the medical literature.

After getting my first case report published as first author, I continued to carry out basic science research experiments with my assigned research mentor at SUNY Downstate. She was a young investigator who depended heavily on her students and research associates to get herself published, promoted, and to increase her chances of acquiring additional research funding. Within the first month of working in her lab, I realized that I would have to get advice from my fellowship director to chart the course for my research project rather than relying on my assigned mentor. I can unequivocally say that I learned basic science techniques and was able to complete my project thanks to the graduate students in the lab. My lab mentor gave me an example of what type of teacher I didn't want to be. That's one thing I took from this experience to help me be a more nurturing mentor in the future.

One time, a 20-liter plastic jug full of pH 7.0 buffer was sitting above a refrigerator. The spigot was hanging over the door of the freezer compartment, but I didn't realize it. When I went to open the freezer door, the buffer bottle came crashing down on me. The spigot lacerated my forehead, and I bled profusely all over my face and neck. I was the only MD in the laboratory, so everyone else around me was panicking, running around looking for a first aid kit. They found only a few pieces of dry gauze and a single bandage left in it. I used the dry gauze to hold pressure over the laceration on my forehead, and I grabbed the phone to call a pediatric ER physician I knew. Next thing I knew, a security guard put me in a wheelchair and took me to the pediatric ER. All along the ride to the ER, so many doctors and medical students were asking, "Dr. Nguyen, are you okay?" But after asking that question, they all walked away like I was going to be fine. I called my husband, who rode his motorcycle from home, about two miles from SUNY Downstate Medical Center. The first thing he did was pull out his cell phone and snap a photo of me covered in dried blood from head to mid-chest. Of course, I had worn a white turtleneck on this day. He then sent the photo to my sisters who lived in Boston. They thought I got into a car accident, but they knew that if my husband was calm enough to snap a photo of me bleeding, it couldn't be too serious. My husband has a calm demeanor no matter how serious the situation may be. Sometimes I get irritated because I can't get him to be serious, but then I just have to laugh about it and try not to take myself too seriously. I guess that's why God put us together, to help us balance out our extreme natures. My husband is one of the reasons I survived my pediatric gastroenterology fellowship and many other challenging situations in my medical career thus far. He tells me if I don't expect too much from people, then I wouldn't have many reasons to be disappointed. When I approach people or situations with this in mind, I get less frustrated and I can strive to be a better person each day.

Thinking back to the "buffer bottle incident," I was somewhat embarrassed at the time, as if I had caused my own medical disaster. Little did I know that the spigot of the buffer jug wasn't supposed to hang over the freezer door. It was the mistake of the laboratory technician. I wasn't upset though; I never hold grudges because we all make mistakes and we all can learn from them. After that incident, I always look twice above any door or cupboard before I open it in case something might come down over my head and assault me.

Dr. Treem and Dr. Schwarz often said to me during fellowship, "Katrina, you always try to make the best out of any situation." In retrospect, I think that attitude comes from the work ethic that my parents instilled in me since childhood. I never took anything for granted and embraced any opportunity given to me.

Completing my medical education was an amazing achievement, but I did come across difficulties that not many medical students have—namely, going against the cultural norms and expectations of a Vietnamese family. I still have vivid memories of the day that my sister Pauline told my family that she was going to Massachusetts for dental school. My parents didn't understand why she couldn't just stay in California for school, and they couldn't accept the concept of Pauline choosing the best dental school she was offered to attend. It just made sense to them for her to choose a dental school close to home like we had done with college. In my view, my parents harbored a lot of resentment with regard to Pauline's decision to move away for dental school. There was an underlying feeling that she had abandoned the family to pursue her personal goals and that she was not contributing to the family's financial and emotional needs.

In 1998, when I was accepted to medical school at the American University of the Caribbean in St. Maarten, I had endured a two-year struggle with getting competitive MCAT scores, juggling the UC Irvine post-baccalaureate program, and working as a research assistant for Dr. Arquilla at the UC Irvine Department of Pathology. My family members did not initially embrace my desire to attend AUC for medical school. They said I was too naïve to go away on my own and that I needed to give up this dream. As you could imagine, I was devastated for many days and prayed to God for guidance. I prayed that if God wanted me to accomplish something for Him with my medical education, then I needed Him to help my parents and brothers understand my wish and allow me to accept AUC's offer for admission. Within a few days, my prayers were answered.

Vietnamese cultural views about women and education made it difficult for my parents to initially understand why any of their daughters would want to pursue anything more than an undergraduate college degree. My parents valued education but also did not think a female should have a higher education than her future spouse. They were always concerned that if their daughters were too highly educated, it may be difficult for them to find a husband. So when Pauline wanted to go to dental school, it was a big deal, especially since she was moving away from home as a single female without a fiancé.

When I decided to pursue a career in medicine, my parents and brothers were appalled that I wanted to move away and spend most of my life training to become a physician. Don't get me wrong, it's an honor for Vietnamese families to say their child is a physician, but most families don't think it would be a woman. Eventually, my family learned to trust my passion for medicine despite my struggles with exams, moving to different cities, applying for training programs, deciding on different job opportunities, and balancing my career and my personal life.

I feel that until Pauline went away to pursue dental school, my parents and older brothers never thought that the women in our family would want to pursue education beyond college. They still held fast to the Vietnamese cultural expectation that women got married, had children, and stayed home to take care of them. They weren't supposed to pursue higher education because it would make it more challenging for them to find a husband.

My family also was not receptive to the idea of us getting married outside the Vietnamese culture or the Catholic faith. I think it's because they had long-held beliefs that Vietnamese culture valued family more and had lower divorce rates. The Catholic faith is also against divorce. However, Pauline and I have helped my family members be more open-minded and less judgmental when it comes to marriage decisions and career choices. They see how we have been able to be happily married and still have fulfilling careers.

I've learned over the years that everything happens for a reason, though we may not understand the reason at the time it happens. The struggle that I experienced to attend medical school has been the driving force that keeps me chasing for more and more opportunities for training. As I have progressed in my training, I realize that it is not where you go to medical school that determines where you end up in your career. It is and always will be how hard you work and how you treat people. That is what matters the most. I was very fortunate to attend an off-shore medical school. It was my first time away from home, and I was so far from home that my family and I were no longer even sharing the same landmass. I had grown up with nine siblings and now I was all alone on a Caribbean island. People came to St. Maarten for fun, not for school. However, I saw firsthand the contrast of poverty (on the Dutch side of the island) and prosperity (on the French side). As a student, I participated in a local health screening, and I saw how fortunate I was to have preventive care in the United States. This experience is forever etched in my mind and heart. Since then, it has remained my dream to provide my medical services to third world countries one day. For now, I donate to Food for the Poor and various disaster relief organizations many times throughout the year.

Nowadays, the undercurrent of resentment about my sister's and my decision to pursue higher education still occasionally has a way to creep back into family conversations. After I left for medical school, my younger sister Mylene moved to Massachusetts to attend school for dental hygiene. She graduated in 2004 and currently lives near Pauline in Hingham, Massachusetts. Pauline, Mylene, and I share a sense of personal guilt over our perceived abandonment of our family. As a way of assuaging our guilt, we spend time with our family whenever possible, on average once or twice a year. We also send them small gifts every now and then, in addition to hosting them whenever they visit us.

There is also resentment on our part when there are expectations from our family. We have all lived on our own for quite awhile now and are no longer accustomed to being told what to do. We feel that we are adults and are independent enough to know how to treat people the way we want to be treated. We have left home and have changed. We want our family to respect our decision-making abilities, give us privacy, and appreciate our efforts to spend quality time with them. We have earned that respect from our family members now that they have seen our many professional achievements, and our bond continues to grow stronger because of it.

6

My First Real Job

**MEDICAL COLLEGE OF GEORGIA
(LATER KNOWN AS AUGUSTA UNIVERSITY)**

*"The best way to find yourself is to lose yourself in
the service of others." —Mahatma Gandhi*

AFTER COMPLETING FELLOWSHIP TRAINING, I was finally able to choose a job that was no longer part of a training program. The world was full of opportunities for me, but I had to find my niche. It was a difficult decision to decline an offer to stay at SUNY Downstate and continue working alongside my mentors. I decided to spread my wings and learn to fly on my own, to develop my style of practice and teaching. I accepted a position as assistant professor of pediatrics at the Medical College of Georgia (MCG) in Augusta and worked there from August 2009 until May 2013. My job description was physician scientist, working part of the time in the basic science research lab and part of the time as a pediatric gastroenterologist.

During my time there, I gradually realized that my passion lies in patient care and not basic science research. I had presented research findings at national meetings annually and wrote a National Institutes of Health (NIH) grant that, though it had high scores, did not receive funding. Some NIH grant reviewers suggested that I consider developing an animal model of eosinophilic esophagitis and studying whether this type of esophageal inflammation can lead to esophageal cancer. In order to do this, I would have to change course towards animal research and work under a different research mentor, something I was not willing to do.

While working in Augusta, I had the opportunity to take care of many children with obesity and its comorbidities such as fatty liver disease, diabetes, hyperlip-idemia, gastroesophageal reflux disease, and obstructive sleep apnea. I was frus-trated as a physician to see these kids and their families in my clinic, because I could give my advice on exercise and nutrition but had no way of knowing if these families would go out there and do what I recommended. Time and again, kids would come back to the clinic having gained more weight and not following any of my recommendations. After a while, I realized the common theme was the lack of access to safe places to exercise, the lack of motivation, and the lack of access to healthy food choices due to socioeconomic issues. At the same time, I observed waste all around me, such as people buying more food than they could eat and grocery stores just throwing away food they couldn't sell. I would see ads constantly on TV on how to lose weight by joining a program, pay this much for food or an exercise product. I thought, Let's get back to the basics. How did people stay lean and fit hundreds of years ago without ever having to pay a dime?

With my Catholic upbringing at heart and a focus on the stewardship message of time, talent, and treasure, I began to think big. I had also observed that in some parts of the world, there is so much waste of plentiful resources that could be balanced with scarcities in other parts of the world. I believed that these resources could be balanced to accomplish the goals of improving children's health. So in September 2012, I held an obesity summit at the Salvation Army Kroc Center in Augusta. I summoned healthcare workers, medical students, and community leaders to discuss my vision on how to combat childhood obesity. After launching a twelve-week childhood obesity intervention program, I encouraged one of my residents, Dr. Jordan Weitzner, to apply for a CATCH grant from the American Academy of Pediatrics, and he was awarded $3,000 to fund the program. In the end, much of that money was returned to AAP because our community orga-nizations stepped up to cover the program's funding so there would be no cost to participants. The program continued in small ways after I left the MCG, but I am most proud of being able to make my vision of a grassroots, community and stewardship-driven obesity intervention program come true. The American Academy of Pediatrics CATCH program statement says, "One pediatrician can make a difference." One of my goals starting in Georgia would be to make an impact on the childhood obesity epidemic.

Around the same time that my NIH grant was turned down for funding, one of my partners decided to leave the clinical practice. He was my division chief but was not a great leader or mentor. He hired me as a physician scientist, but he never protected my time to allow me to achieve these goals. I had to carve out my time in order to provide good care to patients as well as meet deadlines for my research projects in the lab. As hard as I tried to make everything happen, I knew that the stress of work was negatively impacting my marriage. I had to decide whether work or my marriage was more important to me, and I had to learn to find balance in work while also having a meaningful life. All the signs pointed to the fact that MCG was not the right job for me. My husband and I started searching for new jobs, and that's how we ended up moving to Illinois in 2013.

The decision to leave MCG was difficult because I had developed strong collaborations with pediatric surgeons there, including Drs. Charlie Howell, Robyn Hatley and Walter Pipkin. We worked very well together taking care of complex patients with genetic syndromes, feeding difficulties, inflammatory bowel disease, esophageal disorders, liver and gallbladder diseases, and numerous conditions in premature babies. Despite their extensive years of experience in caring for children, the surgeons did not look at my minimal experience as a negative. Instead, they showed respect for my work ethic and compassion for our patients. They gave me a sense of confidence that I contributed more to medicine than just knowledge and skills. They let me know that I had compassion that could not be learned but was innate and seemed to shine through more and more every day. As a young physician, I was honored to learn from among the best physicians at MCG and I am a better physician because of crossing paths with these surgeons.

7

My Second Real Job

ROCKFORD MEMORIAL HOSPITAL
(LATER KNOWN AS MERCYHEALTH)

"We can do no great things, only small things with great love." —St. Teresa of Calcutta

I STARTED MY JOB AT Rockford Memorial Hospital (RMH) in July 2013. I chose to accept the job at RMH because I would join two senior partners who had been working together for about fifteen to twenty years. My division chief and chairman seemed like a nurturing mentor, the complete opposite from my chief at MCG. The job at RMH would be entirely clinical, but I continued to have opportunities to teach medical students and do as much clinical research as I wanted. I was given a faculty appointment as clinical assistant professor at the University of Illinois College of Medicine in Rockford and continued to teach in the clinical setting for students and residents.

Eventually, I also had an opportunity to develop a childhood obesity program in Rockford like I did in Augusta. Childhood obesity intervention was still very dear to my heart and I wanted this to be part of future plans. As you will see, many of my plans since taking on my job at RMH have fallen into place which I believe is through Divine intervention. There's no perfect job, but I know that I found greater work-life balance after moving to the Rockford region.

After starting my job at Rockford Memorial Hospital, I have taken more time to read many non-medical books, especially biographies and memoirs. I particularly enjoyed books by Dr. Ben Carson: *America the Beautiful*, *Gifted Hands*, and *Think Big*. Though the topics in each book varied somewhat, he focused much of his time praising his mom and God. One thing I will always remember from Dr. Carson is the mantra "Do your best and let God do the rest." He has gone from practicing medicine as a neurosurgeon to serving this country as secretary of Housing and Urban Development. He inspired me to think big, to focus on what I can do rather than feel frustrated at things I can't change. His advice crosses my mind each day, especially at work. I think that through charitable work, we can find a balance between our careers and personal lives and learn to appreciate our blessings.

Another area of growth for me after moving to Rockford is my spiritual life. I discovered the writings of Matthew Kelly, founder of Dynamic Catholic. Books such as *Resisting Happiness, Rediscover Jesus, Beautiful Hope, Perfectly Yourself,* and *Why I Love Being Catholic* are just a few of his works that have deepened my relationship with God and encouraged me to be the best version of myself. Working towards a healthier spiritual life has helped me find more joy in my profession as a physician. I realized that I had to renew myself spiritually and emotionally every day to be able to guide my patients towards their path to wellness.

In early 2020, the COVID-19 pandemic became the headline of every news cycle, caused the shutdown of businesses, and changed the practice of healthcare. Elective surgeries were put on hold for several months, crippling the revenue generated by healthcare institutions across the country. In addition to the effects of this pandemic, insurance reimbursement issues in Illinois led my employer to reduce investment in pediatric outpatient and inpatient services, including the closure of the pediatric intensive care unit and reduction in pediatric specialty services. As such, many physicians and nurses were laid off. Although I was offered an opportunity to negotiate a new employment contract, I decided to end my employment here and become independent by working as a *locum tenens* physician. I felt called to serve anywhere I am needed in the U.S. as a pediatric gastroenterologist. I also wanted to work independently so that I could think and share my political, social and religious beliefs without being censored.

8

The Formation of Faithful-2-Fitness

"We make a living by what we get, but we make a life
by what we give." —Winston Churchill

A FTER LEAVING THE MEDICAL COLLEGE of Georgia in May 2013, I still carried with me the passion to fight childhood obesity. I learned through researching online that a 2011 Gallup survey showed that Rockford was the fourth most obese metropolitan area in the United States. A light bulb went off in my head! God had a mission for me and part of His plan was for me to come to Rockford. On November 6, 2014, Faithful-2-Fitness was formed, and on April 18, 2015, the first childhood obesity intervention program was launched in Rockford. Since then, we have had between thirty and fifty families each year develop healthier lifestyles through diet and exercise.

During my life's journey, I have often felt that God puts people in our lives for a specific reason. We may not understand the reason when it happens, but eventually He will reveal His purpose later in life.

Christy Flagler is one of those people. She is the mother of one of the patients when I worked at MCG. Christy called her daughter a miracle baby after she survived a long course in the NICU there. As a teenager, Christy's daughter was brought to my clinic for a second opinion after her first set of doctors could not make a diagnosis. I made the correct diagnosis, and her condition improved after an elimination diet. However, because of her medical problems prior to seeing me, she had missed lots of school and had to attend an alternative high school in order to graduate with her class.

In early 2014, I was envisioning creating an obesity intervention program in

Rockford. In fact, I wanted to establish a nonprofit organization whose mission was to fight childhood obesity across America. Part of creating this nonprofit was obtaining trademarks for the organization's name and logo, something I felt was so overwhelming that I didn't know where to begin. While sitting in my office at Rockford Memorial Hospital contemplating this idea, I received a phone call from Christy's daughter. She was going off to college and wanted to join a sorority. Because she had attended an alternative school, the sorority needed a letter of recommendation from a physician explaining how her medical issues affected her high school experience. I agreed to write the letter so I spoke to Christy, who then emailed me the details I needed. As I finished reading Christy's email on my computer, I looked at her signature line, which stated, "Trademark Specialist." I have no doubt that it was definitely Divine intervention that brought us back together. Christy was back in my life to help me carry out God's mission for me. Thanks to assistance from Christy's employer, the law firm Kilpatrick Townsend, Faithful-2-Fitness received a registered trademark on April 26, 2016. Kilpatrick Townsend continues to provide pro bono services as intellectual property counsel to Faithful-2-Fitness.

It is worth mentioning that the formation of Faithful-2-Fitness might not have happened at all. One weekend in September 2014, as I was approaching the deadline to submit my trademark paperwork for the Faithful-2-Fitness logo, I was exercising at Peak Sports Club. A few days later, I had left lower quadrant abdominal pain. The pain was like a tugging sensation that was exacerbated with bending or twisting of my trunk. I never had appendicitis, though I would imagine it's the same pain but on the left side instead.

At first, a CT scan was suspicious for diverticulitis, a condition involving inflammation in the intestines. I was instructed to be on a clear liquid diet and take two oral antibiotics for about two-to-three weeks. However, the pain got worse, along with nausea and lower gastrointestinal symptoms. By day six of symptoms, I went to the ER for evaluation. A surgeon saw me and had another CT scan done to check for bowel perforation. The repeat CT scan showed acute epiploic appendagitis, a rare diagnosis involving a benign, non-surgical inflammatory process that affects small, fat filled sacs along the surfaces of the lower intestinal tract. These sacs can be acutely inflamed as a result of torsion or venous thrombosis. In retrospect, I think the appendagitis may have been caused by the vigorous exercise I did the previous weekend.

I did not require any surgery for my abdominal pain, but I was hospitalized, halting my work on Faithful-2-Fitness and jeopardizing my ability to make the trademark deadline. While I was in the hospital, I also experienced a severe adverse reaction to a pain medication called Dilaudid, which manifested as severe vertigo. It started on a Saturday morning, which made me concerned about missing Mass on Sunday. I asked the nurse to contact St. Bernadette Catholic Church for someone to bring me communion. A few hours after I received communion and prayed to God for recovery, I suddenly felt better and was able to walk around with my IV pole without any pain or nausea. I called the surgeon, who agreed to discharge me on Saturday evening. I made it to church the next morning to praise God for healing me. After my recovery, I got back to work on Faithful-2-Fitness and was able to meet the deadline to file for the trademark.

While pursuing trademark status, I also had to pursue nonprofit status in order to establish Faithful-2-Fitness as a registered 501(c)(3) charitable organization. Being new to the Rockford area and not having many friends in the legal field, I was at a loss as to where to begin. I asked my partners in the medical practice, but nobody had good connections that wouldn't cost me a fortune. I prayed for God to guide me to the right people that would help me to fulfill His mission.

One night, I was talking to my husband about needing to find an attorney to establish nonprofit status for Faithful-2-Fitness. He reminded me that he worked with Dr. Frank Nicolosi, who is also an attorney. Dr. Nicolosi referred us to his nephew, Phil Nicolosi, who agreed to be the registered agent for Faithful-2-Fitness. Phil has been extremely devoted to making sure Faithful-2-Fitness meets all the legal obligations necessary to maintain its nonprofit status, which was granted on January 5, 2015.

From the first meeting with Phil Nicolosi, I told him that I was looking for a company to design a website for Faithful-2-Fitness. Once again, there had to be Divine intervention for me to have picked Phil as the attorney for Faithful-2- Fitness, because he shared that his brother, Eli, is the owner of Astute Web Group, which does website design. Within a few weeks, I met with Eli and his assistant, Nicole Arand. They took time to hear my vision for Faithful-2-Fitness and my ideas for the website. Within one month, the website was built and launched. They also created a Facebook page and had business cards and T-shirts printed. They were on board from the beginning to help me share the vision of Faithful-2-Fitness with the Rockford community and beyond. They have also provided their services free-of-charge to make our annual 5K event held every August—"Fight Obesity: Walk with Me"—a success. I am forever grateful to Astute Web Group for helping me share Faithful-2-Fitness with the world. I don't know if I will ever be able to repay them for their immense kindness.

Once the groundwork was laid for the establishment of Faithful-2-Fitness, I began the process of recruiting community partnerships that could help me carry out my vision. I wanted to find partners that were passionate about helping children develop healthier lifestyles, and I envisioned a model of an obesity intervention program that could be replicated in any community across America. Based on my experience in establishing the obesity intervention program in Augusta, I had a model in mind that at minimum consisted of a fitness center, dietitian, chef/cook, hospital, and a grocery store.

With this in mind, I contacted various fitness centers in the Rockford area. After being denied by several of them, I wanted to give up. I even contacted the local YMCA, whose director told me, "Why would the YMCA, which is a nonprofit, want to help another nonprofit?" Needless to say, I was taken aback by this response.

I still truly believe that God was testing my perseverance to accomplish this task. I prayed to God to guide me to the right people and places if it was His will. I decided to contact the gym where I worked out, Peak Sports Club, which is considered a high-end fitness center in the Rockford area. I scheduled a meeting with manager Tony Teunissen and group fitness director Wendy Beggs. Before the meeting, I prayed that the Holy Spirit would guide me to be able to clearly convey my vision and touch the hearts of people to join me on this project. After less than one hour, Peak Sports Club was on board to launch the first community-based childhood obesity intervention program in Rockford. Ever since the beginning, the staff at Peak Sports Club have always been very welcoming and kind to our participants. They make me feel that they are honored and blessed to be associated with Faithful-2-Fitness.

My next step was to find someone in the culinary field who could assist with cooking classes. When I was in Georgia, local chef Edward Mendoza and Wildtree sales representative Janette Schultz were my go-to people for this task. I contacted Janette because Wildtree is a national company specializing in healthy cooking techniques and products. She immediately signed on and helped connect me with Wildtree employees in the Illinois and Wisconsin area. I then tried to reach out to chefs that were suggested to me by my co-workers and acquaintances. Once again, despite many phone calls and attempts to schedule meetings, I could never find any chef who was committed to help.

One weekend while on call at the hospital, I talked to a pediatric nurse named Cassie about Faithful-2-Fitness and my struggles to find a culinary partner. She mentioned Jim McIlroy, who is the owner of Food-4-Fuel, a local business that prepares healthy, portion-controlled meals for health-conscious clients. I called Jim a few times and we finally met up at the Starbucks on Bell School Road in Rockford. We shared our common passion to improve the health of Rockford and discussed how we could help each other further this mission. After about an hour, Food-4-Fuel signed on to become a community partner of Faithful-2-Fitness. Little did Jim know that God had bigger plans for me to be a part of his life a few years down the line.

In the summer of 2019, Wildtree sales representatives could no longer provide meal prep classes for our program because of some changes at the corporate level. I was initially concerned about how to continue making the cooking class possible for our program. At the same time, I knew that if God wanted me to continue my mission to fight obesity, He would make a way for it to happen. Fortunately, Stacie Woodworth, a Wildtree sales representative who had briefly volunteered for Faithful-2-Fitness, decided to sign up as a representative for a new company called Epicure. I researched Epicure and learned that their mission to help families eat healthier aligned well with the goals of Faithful-2-Fitness. Since August 2019, Stacie has helped me organize cooking classes for our program and also provides similar classes in various households throughout Illinois.

From the beginning of establishing Faithful-2-Fitness, I searched long and hard to find a grocery store in Rockford that would partner with us by donating gift cards we could use to buy groceries for cooking classes. I was denied by many stores either in person, by email or by regular mail. Just when I was going to give up, a new grocery store called Meijer opened in Rockford, less than a mile from where I lived at the time. I was initially hesitant to ask for Meijer's support because I thought a new store wouldn't have as many resources to donate. However, I spoke to one of the physicians in my practice who used to live in Michigan, where Meijer is based, and he told me that Meijer is very good about doing things for the community. I called the store manager who gave me some tips on the application process for charitable support requests. Meijer signed on as a partner with Faithful-2-Fitness and has covered the cost of groceries for our cooking classes since April 2015. In return, we take the participants of Faithful-2-Fitness through Meijer for a tour and mini-shopping trip for healthy foods about once every twelve weeks. This is our small way of giving back to Meijer for what the store offers our families.

A culinary-related community partner was added for the Rockford program in September 2015. I believe that if children understand where food comes from and learn how to prepare meals, they would be more willing to eat it. I wanted to find a farm nearby that could serve as a site for nutrition education. Through an internet search of farms near the Rockford area, I found Angelic Organics Learning Center in Caledonia, Illinois, about twenty minutes from Loves Park where Peak Sports Club is located. Without hesitation, the farm's learning center became a partner and gave Faithful-2-Fitness a discount to bring families there for guided farm tours. The farm tour is also an opportunity for kids to take walks in nature and view being physically active as something fun and not a chore.

I would be remiss to not mention Christine Gillette, a dietitian who worked with me at the hospital. She has been a passionate volunteer for our program from the time we launched the first program in April 2015. She provides informal nutrition lessons for the kids and parents at the end of exercise classes, and she helps with the cooking classes by providing commentary about the health benefits of different ingredients used in our dishes. She also leads the grocery store tours at Meijer, where kids are allowed to choose healthy items that fit a budget funded by Faithful-2-Fitness. My heart is full every time we complete a grocery store tour. Seeing the smiles on the kids' faces is what makes all the hard work so fulfilling.

After completing the first year of programs with Faithful-2-Fitness, my next goal was to put together an annual 5K event annually to raise awareness about our organization. I am happy to say that

Having a healthy society is a key to having a successful society. I have been fortunate that I have always been involved in athletics my whole life and that has kept me in good health, but it takes a program like Faithful-2-Fitness to bring that to our entire community. I really like that it starts with the families and the kids to create healthy lifestyles. I think it is very important to have a program like Faithful-2-Fitness all across this country because having a healthy nation leads to having a wealthy and successful nation. I thank Katrina for her dedication to this program; our city appreciates her commitment.

–Mayor Greg Jury
Loves Park, Illinois

on August 13, 2016, we hosted our first 5K event, called "Fight Obesity: Walk with Me." Rockford mayor Larry Morrissey kicked off our event with some encouraging words to show support for Faithful-2-Fitness. The local media, including TV station WREX and *The Rockford Register Star*, provided publicity for the 5K. We had more than 140 participants and 25 sponsors. Most importantly, we raised awareness about what we do as a service to the Rockford community. We have continued hosting our annual 5K event every year in August to fundraise and raise awareness on our work to make a difference in the childhood obesity epidemic. Participation in our annual 5K event has exceeded 250 people including adults and kids. Since August 2017, Mayor Greg Jury of Loves Park has been the speaker at our 5K events and been an ardent supporter of our work to improve children's health.

9

Light of the World Retreat
and Faith Community

WHEN I WAS GROWING UP in California, people around us used to make us feel like our family was the epitome of holiness. I recall that in college a Korean girl approached me while I was sitting at the food court at the University of California, Irvine, trying to eat lunch quickly before my next class. Without any hesitation about interrupting my lunch hour, she sat down next to me at the booth and said, "Do you know God?" What a ridiculous question, I thought. With two brothers who are Catholic priests, how much more about God did I need to know? I turned to her after a few minutes of her preaching and said, "I think you shouldn't waste time on me. I already know God quite well." With that, she left me alone to finish my lunch.

In March 2014, after living in Rockford for about eight months, I began to assimilate into the community. It was Lent and after leaving Mass one weekend, I saw a flyer about the Light of the World retreat, a weekend program offered in Catholic parishes in more than thirty states. Wow, a retreat for Catholics—what a novel idea! While contemplating whether I should attend, I also wondered if Rockford was going to be a place I would live for a long time, if not forever. Of all the job opportunities out there, why did I choose Rockford? I felt a tugging at my heart to go to the retreat. It turned out that I was off the weekend of the retreat, so I decided to go. But after I signed up, Marconi told me he had made an appointment with our CPA that same weekend to file our taxes. It was tempting for me to use this as an excuse to back out of the retreat, but again I felt the tugging to make the commitment. I told my husband I would still go to the retreat and take a one-hour break to meet the CPA with him.

The decision to go to that retreat has forever changed my life. It has reaffirmed that God brought me to Rockford for a reason, whether it may be for a short time or forever. I had to surrender my life to God and trust that there is a purpose for me in Rockford.

I have since learned that Light of the World retreat format was started in Rockford. After the retreat, I was given guidance to lead a new faith community. After much prayer and reflection, I volunteered to lead a faith community about two or three times a month in prayer, study of scripture, spiritual edification, and fellowship. I began to voluntarily go to Eucharistic adoration once a week on Wednesday afternoons. I have never in my life looked forward so much to spending time in prayer, Eucharistic adoration, study of scripture, and meditation. I wake up each morning and go to bed each night asking myself, "Have I prayed today?"

Through the Light of the World retreat, I met Dr. Edward Santos, a pathologist at OSF St. Anthony Medical Center in Rockford. He told me about the Catholic Medical Association, a national organization that has a Rockford guild. Because I wanted to keep what I learned and experienced at the retreat alive in both my spiritual and professional lives, I decided to become a member. I finally realized that the practice of medicine and the practice of Catholicism did not have to be a dichotomy; there was a lot of overlap between the healing of the body and the healing of the soul. After joining the Catholic Medical Association, my perspective on the practice of medicine also changed. Rather than feeling like every struggle or success was only due to my own skill and knowledge, I viewed the practice of medicine as a privilege given to me from God. I saw that God was using me to serve the world and lift up people who are suffering. I learned to ask God for help in every patient encounter and to thank Him for every accomplishment. I learned not to gloat about achievements but rather be grateful for opportunities and blessings.

Many years ago, before attending Light of the World Retreat or joining the Catholic Medical Association, I attended Mass at a mission church during a trip for a medical conference. I visited the gift shop of the church after Mass and found a laminated card that said, "Prayer for the Physician and Surgeon." The prayer goes like this:

> *"Dear Cosmas and Damian, I pray that through your intercession with our Heavenly Father I may be inspired by Divine compassion for my patients. Give skill to my hand, clear vision to my mind, kindness and*

> *sympathy to my heart. Give me singleness of purpose, strength to lift at*
> *least a part of the burden of my suffering fellowmen and a true realization*
> *of the privilege that is mine. Take from me all guile and worldliness so*
> *that with the simple faith of a child, I can rely on my Lord. Amen."*

One day in Rockford, I found the laminated card stashed away in some dusty boxes at home. Since completing the Light of the World retreat, I say this prayer during my drive to work or during breaks at the office. I have a copy of the prayer taped to my computer monitor. Ever since I took the time to pray in the spirit of this prayer each morning, even my difficult days at work have become pleasant or at least bearable. When I am having a tough day, I retreat to my office, take a deep breath and ask for God's help. Learning to incorporate prayer into my workday has changed my outlook on life and my career. With every decision I make for myself and my patients, I pray about it more often than I ever did in the past, and I feel this has made me a better physician.

10

The People Who Shaped Me

"Live today the way you want to be remembered
tomorrow." —Dillon Burroughs

Vietnamese proverb:	*Translation:*
Công cha như núi Thái Sơn	The good deeds of Father are as great as Mount Thai Son
Nghĩa mẹ như nước trong nguồn chảy ra	The virtue of Mother is as bountiful as spring water gushing from its source
Một lòng thờ mẹ kính cha	Wholeheartedly is Mother to be revered and Father respected
Cho tròn chữ hiếu mới là đạo con	So that the child's way may be accomplished.

DAD

My dad was the loving parent but not the disciplinarian in our family. We learned to ask Mom for permission first and then seek Dad's approval. We had no doubt that Dad would say yes if Mom did. Dad would ask us if we had talked it over with Mom, and if we had, then he would say yes to just about everything. Deep down, I think he trusted my mom's judgment.

Our family was not known for public displays of affection, but we always had each other's backs. Things didn't change until some of us moved away from home and came back during special occasions or holidays. My dad was the first one in the family who showed outward affection for me and my sisters, Pauline and Mylene, since we were the girls who lived far away from home. He was not afraid to hug and kiss us. When he did it the first time, he was teased by my mom and siblings, and we were all a little embarrassed.

My dad wanted to make sure we were happy and liked to give gifts away to his kids and grandkids for various occasions. That was another way for him to demonstrate his love. He wanted his kids to have no doubt they were loved and that we were constantly on his mind. My dad often included us in his favorite hobby: fishing. Ever since I was in elementary school, my dad would ask each of the girls if we wanted to go pier fishing with him at one of the Southern California beaches. He made a fishing kit from a crushed soda can with a fishing line wrapped around it and a bunch of hooks on the line. He created fake bait using shiny fabric strands from the clothes taken from our dolls. These proved to be the best bait for catching any type of fish, because the shiny strands created a shimmering effect in the water below that attracted fish. My dad rarely bought live bait.

Once we demonstrated that we could handle the soda can fishing kit, he taught us how to use the fishing rod. Eventually, we learned how to hook bait, take fish off the hook, and clean them. My dad left the cooking of the fish to my mom, who then passed on recipes for preparing fish to the kids. To this day, a lot of my friends are amazed to hear that I enjoy fishing and know how to clean and cook the fish that I catch.

Dad was a creative person but he did not need special materials for his crafty projects. He liked to create life-sized nativity scenes in our living room for the Christmas season. He used bamboo to assemble the basic frame for the stable. Each year he would change the design around the bamboo frame to give a different appearance to the nativity scene. Some years there were many colorful lights, and other years

Me with Dad's annual nativity scene

the scene was dimly lit. Sometimes, he shaped brown paper bags into rocks and spray-painted them silver to create a stone appearance around the bamboo frame. Sometimes there were strands of tinsel spread over the frame to mimic icicles. We looked forward every year to dad's nativity scene and he was always proud to share his project with us as a way to add joy to the Christmas season.

Me and Dad at my first communion

One of the most endearing memories about my dad is that he frequently asked me and my sisters to pluck graying whiskers from his beard. As he got older, we started to pluck his gray hair too until his hair was all gray. Sometimes he would give us some money for doing these tasks, but we never expected it. It was just father-daughter bonding time and each of us cherished being Daddy's little girl.

Whenever any of us was sad, my dad was always there with a sympathetic ear. My siblings and I knew that our dad loved us with all his heart. He seemed bothered watching us being disciplined by our mom. It broke his heart when his kids felt alone or hurt, so he often took that first step to say he understood and that he is sorry to see us going through a difficult time. My dad helped my mom strike a fine balance between discipline and love.

Although my dad never received any formal education because of his family's poverty, he taught us to love one another, to respect elders, to work hard, to be responsible, and most of all, to trust in God. No amount of education anywhere in the world can teach us all these values.

Around August 2017, Dad's health began to decline. His appetite was poor, he lost weight, bled from hemorrhoids, and developed chronic kidney disease. He also developed intermittent chest pain in the middle of the night and early morning. Because I was the only physician in the family, I was asked by some of my siblings to help figure out what was causing Dad's health problems. I became very involved in his healthcare decisions and found him a new primary care physician who was able to help get our family more answers.

On March 31, 2018, which was Holy Saturday, Dad spoke repeatedly to my sisters by phone about forgiveness and the Gospel in which St. Peter asked Jesus how many times a person should forgive someone. The answer Jesus gave was seventy times seven. On April 1, the morning of Easter Sunday, Dad was hospitalized due to a heart attack. Because of his age and other medical conditions, he was considered high risk for cardiac catheterization or bypass surgery. He decided to accept only medical (not surgical) treatment as long as his body could still function. He chose to spend time preparing spiritually for the end of his life.

On the evening of Easter Sunday, my sister Hong and I spent the night with dad in the cardiac intensive care unit (CICU) at the University of California Irvine Medical Center. From that night until the next morning, Dad repeatedly told us to "open the gates." Each time he uttered these words, Hong and I would tell him, "Dad, there are no gates to open, you are in the hospital." We thought he was hallucinating or was disoriented due to his hospitalization. However, the more we tried to explain to him that he was in the hospital, the more Dad would say, "Open the gates, there are people waiting for me." It was not until after he had passed away and we were home sitting down for dinner on the night of his death that we realized dad was most likely referring to the "gates" of Heaven.

Within the last hour before Dad took his last breath, he said these words in Vietnamese to all his family members gathered in prayer at his bedside: "St. Peter is the only saint that matters. Pray to St. Peter, and if you have time then pray to the other saints." His eyes were closed and he looked unconscious, but these were the words that were clearly spoken from his lips.

My dad passed away on April 2, 2018. I miss him dearly, but I try to reflect on the memories we have made together. Father's Day will be hard for a while because I got married on Father's Day weekend, so every wedding anniversary will also be a reminder of Dad. After his death, I reflected on how many things make me feel very connected to Dad that I hadn't taken time to recognize before his passing. Marconi and I had gone on our first date on January 25, 2003, which also happened to be my dad's birthday. Because I had a more Americanized wedding than my other siblings, I was the first girl who Dad walked down the aisle. I grew up being told I was his mini-me. I chose the song "My Girl" for my father-daughter dance and my dad provided lots of "entertainment" for the wedding guests with his dance moves. I loved this song for our dance because of its happy, upbeat music and lyrics and because it reminds me of one of my favorite wedding movies, *Father of the Bride*.

Dad's passing taught me a lot about suffering, death, spirituality, and the afterlife. If I ever had any doubts about the afterlife and the connection of humans on Earth to the souls in purgatory, my dad's passing removed all those doubts. Between his statement of "open the gates" and his declaration to pray to St. Peter, I firmly believe that dad was on his path to Heaven, if he is not already there. I pray every day, not only for Dad, but also to him, to ask him to guide me and our family to do God's will and to bring sinners back to God.

It is noteworthy that the day dad passed away was the Monday of Divine Mercy week, which liturgically emphasizes God's mercy and forgiveness. The importance of mercy and forgiveness were messages that Dad repeated to my sisters before he was hospitalized.

Dad chose me to be his agent in his power of attorney for healthcare, and I tried my best to honor his wishes regarding his medical care until his last breath. Carrying out this role was a challenging experience because I had so many siblings who all wanted a say in his care, and this was the first time we had a death in the family. I repeatedly said that I was honoring Dad's wishes, not making decisions for him. I struggled with a recurring thought that maybe I had let Dad go too soon, or at least that some people in my family may have thought I didn't try hard enough to keep him alive longer.

On April 15, 2018, I was sleeping on Dad's old bed with my sister Mylene. Before I went to bed, I prayed to Dad to give me a sign that he was fine with everything I had done for his medical care while I carried out his healthcare wishes. That night until the next morning as I slept on Dad's bed, I had a dream in which my family was at a picnic. My mom, my second oldest brother Tuan, and I were crossing a bamboo bridge. I could hear many other family members in the background but could not see all of them. As my mom, Tuan, and I got more than halfway across the bridge, only I saw Dad fishing. He was casting his line and reeling it in repeatedly. Once I woke up, I realized that Dad had given me the message I was looking for—that he was happy on the other side of the "bridge" doing what he loves: fishing. I felt so much joy knowing dad gave me a message in such a meaningful way.

My dad's CICU room number was 7222. On April 22, as my husband and I finished breakfast at the Waffle Shop in Loves Park, Illinois, I was telling Marconi about the numbers 7 and 2 that I kept seeing show up as a reminder of dad. My husband jokingly said that I'm going to walk out to my car after breakfast and start seeing 7s and 2s on my license plate in the parking lot. Well, it turns out that the same license plate that I've had since moving to Illinois in June 2013 was R73-2227. I had traded in my car in February 2016 and decided to keep this license plate on my new car for no apparent reason. I think I now know the reason I couldn't let go of this license plate. The recognition that my license plate number is a mirror image of my dad's CICU room number has made me feel that Dad will always have my back everywhere I go. I feel comfort thinking of this when I step into my car each day, where I usually say my morning prayers on the way to work.

I met Angie Scordato, an artist in Rockford, when I helped her son during the first program of Faithful-2-Fitness. After having the dream of my dad, I decided I wanted to have it turned into a painting. When I reached out to Angie to ask her to consider painting my dream, she chose 7/22 at 2 p.m. for me to meet her for this project. When I told Angie the significance of our meeting date and also showed her my license plate, she was overwhelmed and later told me that she felt that my dad truly helped her convey my dream into her painting. The original painting now hangs in my dining room, and I intensely admire it whenever I miss my dad. The painting was eventually reproduced digitally nine times by Camera Craft in Rockford onto smaller canvas replicas. I presented the nine copies as gifts to my nine siblings as a memory of Dad on the first anniversary of his passing into eternal life.

The painting of my dream

Each of us grieves in different ways. My dad's tombstone has an inscription that came to my mind right after he passed away. It reads, "A man of few words, his love spoke volumes." Every time we visit Dad at the cemetery, this saying summarizes how we will always remember him. Writing this memoir and sharing my stories about Dad during his life and my connections to him after his death is one way I am learning to heal from this tremendous loss. I decided a couple of months after Dad's passing to build a memory garden in the backyard of my house in honor of him. I love to plant vegetables and I already had several raised beds in my yard, so I decided to add four rectangular raised beds and a circular raised bed. The circular bed was in the middle with the four rectangular beds radiating outward to form the shape of a cross. I planted a Chinese blue wisteria tree in the circular bed and used the other beds to grow vegetables. I also ordered a bench made in Vietnam from ballah wood as part of the memory garden. An additional concrete bench in the garden was given to me as a gift from my friend, Christine Gillette. The concrete bench has the inscription: "Our family chain is broken and nothing seems the same, but as God calls us one by one the chain will link again." These two benches are placed diagonally from each other. At night, LED lights brighten the benches and the wisteria tree. I love tending to Dad's garden, and I look forward to planting season every year so that I can spend more time there to show him that I might have inherited Mom's green thumb.

MOM

My family would not be as orderly and accomplished as we are today were it not for my mother. She is a strong woman, physically and emotionally. She was the youngest child in her family and became an orphan by the time she was seven years old. She lived with one of her sisters until she was seventeen years old, which is when she married my father, who was twenty-two, through somewhat of an arranged marriage. About five years later, my oldest brother Hien was born.

Because my dad was the oldest in his family, he had a great deal of responsibility to care for his family. By marrying him, my mom stepped into the role of providing for the rest of my dad's family. She suffered physical and emotional abuse from my paternal grandmother very early in her marriage and this continued until my paternal grandparents passed away. My mom says that she forgives, but it is hard to forget all the suffering she endured early in her marriage.

When I was in junior high school, my mom often told stories about her experience as a daughter-in-law in Vietnam. My dad was the oldest in his family and so he played an important role in financially supporting the extended family. He owned a fishing business, had many people working for him, and was out at sea for months at a time. His lack of presence on a daily basis led to my mom's sense of abandonment and made her vulnerable to physical and emotional abuse from her mother-in-law. My mom recalled the countless times that her mother-in-law would hit her with a thick bamboo stick, often because she didn't answer relatives with the right words, pour tea the right way, or do her chores in a timely fashion or to her mother-in-law's satisfaction. Whenever my father returned home from his fishing trips, my grandmother would tell stories about my mother's supposed disrespect and misbehavior while he was away. This added fuel to the fire and made it challenging for Mom to learn to be loved.

My mother often shared her stories of abuse whenever my sisters came to visit after they got married. My mom would be the shoulder to cry on for my sisters and was sympathetic to their marital challenges. My mom and sisters bonded through their common pain.

Over the years, I continue to observe how each of my siblings's marriages have unfolded. I want to take the opportunity through this book to bring to light many topics that are taboo for discussion among the Vietnamese community. For instance, the Vietnamese paternalistic culture seems to embrace the idea that women are subservient to their husbands. Because of such views, Vietnamese women suffer greatly but silently, trying to avoid causing shame to their extended families by preventing divorce. I want to help Vietnamese women feel empowered to speak their minds, become educated, feel that they are equal partners in a marriage, and have no fear to get out and get help when they are being physically, emotionally, or psychologically abused.

I read a book by an inspirational speaker John O'Leary called *On Fire*. He shared seven choices to ignite a radically inspiring life. In the book, he says, "Fear and love are two great motivators. While fear suffocates, love liberates." He shares that relationships cannot be built on fear, because there is always one person wanting to be accepted as normal. Until each person in a relationship can fully love the other person for who he/she is, the relationship will not flourish. I think this is sound advice to help improve the relationships of Vietnamese families so that the paternalistic views do not dominate.

Me and Mom at my first communion

I remembered in high school when I stayed after school to work on a science fair project for a couple of months. Because of the time it took to get all this work done, I kept missing my bus ride home. There was nobody at home to give me a ride, so I either walked or found the city bus that dropped me off near my house. One day, I got home really late because I got lost walking home and got on the wrong city bus, which stopped much further from home. By the time I got into the house, it was pitch dark. My mom had a wooden stick and was ready to spank me. I knelt down on the carpet and was ready for the spanking. My mom kept asking me where I was and what I was doing. I told her the whole truth: "I was working on my science fair project!" But the whipping didn't stop. I was so angry and bitter that I was being punished and grounded for working so hard on my science fair project.

A few months later, I was putting the final touches on my three-panel presentation for the Villa Park High School science fair competition. My parents weren't able to attend the award ceremony, but my brother Huy came. At the end of the night and after many judges had passed through the aisles of projects on display, I was awarded the Sweepstakes Trophy, the highest honor for this annual event. I was featured on the front page of the school newspaper and I was so proud to show it to my mom. Although we never spoke about how she physically hurt me for being a good student, I knew that she began to trust me from that point on. I don't remember being disciplined for missing the school bus again.

Another time, I recalled getting my mom's permission to go see *Phantom of the Opera* with my college friends. My friends and I got all dressed up for the event. I was at the mercy of my friends driving me to the show and getting me home in a timely fashion. Back in the early '90s, not many of us had cell phones, and it was hard to find a public phone in a safe area of Los Angeles. So even after telling Mom that I should be home around 11:00 p.m., I ended up not getting home until 2:00 a.m. My mom was worried to death and I got another spanking. I was grounded for months, but I felt that deep down my mom knew I was a good kid in a situation that I had no control over. My mom learned later that once I was able to drive, I was very prompt, kept my promises and did my best to make sure she didn't have to worry about me too much.

So nowadays, when people ask me about corporal punishment, I have mixed feelings. I believe that corporal punishment should not be allowed in schools. There definitely should never be any physical abuse of children or adults for any reason. But I feel that parents should be allowed to discipline their children if the purpose is to make sure they stay on the right track and not follow the wrong crowd. My mom never received any formal education because her family could not afford it, but she valued the education of her children and made sure each of us stayed on the right path and made the most of the opportunity to learn, even if that meant using physical discipline to make a statement.

I would say that during our childhood and most of our adulthood, Dad was closer to his girls and Mom closer to her boys. After Dad passed away, all of us learned to develop a closer bond with Mom the best we could. We are all still grieving in different ways, but I can't imagine how hard it must be for Mom to lose her spouse of sixty-four years. They had their ups and downs like all married couples do, but their love ran deep and I pray that my and my siblings' marriages will endure the passage of time like our parents' did.

A TRIBUTE TO MY NINE SIBLINGS

"To whom much is given, much will be required." —Luke 12:48

In many ways, we are just like any other Vietnamese or Catholic family (except for the two Catholic priests, of course). We are faced with the same issues that other Vietnamese families face. Each of us has struggled with the paternalistic aspects of Vietnamese culture, marital challenges, ethnic identity, the clash of cultures, generational gap, poverty, physical and emotional abuse. We face the same concerns as many Catholics, such as morality, spirituality, and tolerance for other religions. Sometimes these issues affect each one of us more than we are willing to acknowledge. Now as a woman in her forties, I know for a fact that having two brothers who are Catholic priests has influenced my life in ways that most other Vietnamese Catholics would not have likely experienced.

When I was growing up, my friends would often tell me they wished they had a younger or older brother or sister. I would say, "I have all of those combinations,

My entire family celebrating my oldest brother's ordination to the priesthood

so you are welcome to come over and borrow one any time." As I matured and left home to pursue my dreams, I often reflected on how blessed I was to have each of my siblings. They each play an important role in shaping who I have become and taught me how to share my blessings with others. As one of ten children, I learned very quickly not to be selfish, and I believe this trait has carried me very far in my life as well as in my career in medicine.

I felt very lonely when I left home because I grew up surrounded by so much love, mixed in with lots of drama, which should not be unexpected in a large family. I missed the daily conversations at dinner, bowling nights, going to the movies together, and dining out with my extended family. We always talked more than we ate during gatherings, usually telling each other all the good and bad things that happened to us that day. I wasn't very talkative as a child, but I enjoyed listening to all the fascinating stories my parents and siblings had to share. I often thought that one day I would have interesting things to share when my life was more exciting.

Not only has my life been an exciting journey, it has been blessed and fulfilling because of my siblings constantly making memories with me. We have our drama and disagreements, just like any other family, but we always have each other's backs. One thing we don't do is exploit each other for fame or money. We are always there to do all we can to prevent other people from exploiting us.

My Brothers

Rev. Hien Minh Nguyen
Born November 16, 1957, in Vietnam
Profession: Catholic priest

Hien has been the rock of our family for as long as I can remember. My family is unlike other families in which the parents made the rules and the kids followed them. Hien was and still is the father figure in our household, especially because my dad was always very soft-spoken. Hien is skeptical and has a watchful eye to make sure other people do not take advantage of our family. Hien has struck the balance between being cautious but trusting, learning over time that his family members will do the right thing.

Hien is the most well travelled person in the family. He is fluent in Spanish, French, Italian, English, and Vietnamese. Because of his training as a priest, he also has knowledge of Latin. He is one of those "language people" who doesn't have to live in a country daily to achieve fluency and can carry on a conversation in any of the languages above. I took six years of French from junior high to high school, including French literature. Though I can read, write, and understand French, I cannot carry on an impromptu conversation. I greatly admire his language skills.

He has often served as the problem solver because my parents and siblings turned to him for guidance in difficult situations. Through his vocation as a priest, he studied Canon Law in Rome for four years, something that aided him in critical thinking and problem solving. We had confidence in him to logically point out every problem and present options for resolution, taking into account cultural, ethical, and religious issues that were important to everyone involved. I can't imagine how much pressure there must be for him to take on this role for our family when we face challenges together. Whether or not we all agree with his diplomatic resolutions on family issues, we all appreciate that he calls family meetings to try to solve problems rather than letting things linger endlessly. He knows that we can only heal once there is a resolution, and he is always ready to take the first step.

Hien has experienced many trials in his life, but he has always demonstrated a commitment to serving God until the day God calls him home. He has a grateful heart and he has taught all of my siblings to be more grateful rather than focus on our adversities.

* * *

Tuan Anh Nguyen
Born June 26, 1958, in Vietnam
Education: BS in electrical engineering
Profession: electrical engineer

Tuan is my second oldest brother. He got married in 1988 and has two children. He is a soft-spoken man who has many of my father's qualities. All of us have often felt the need to be protective of him. He suffered transient ischemic attacks, or "mini-strokes," in his thirties and forties, much of which occurred during times when there was a lot of stress in his life.

Despite what appears to others as weakness, his soft-spoken nature is probably what has helped him endure many challenges in life. What Tuan has taught me is that we all have strengths and weaknesses. Tuan helped each of us recognize our own weaknesses so that we can work to strengthen those areas of our lives that need to change.

* * *

Rev. Huy Nhat Nguyen
Born July 4, 1962, in Vietnam
Profession: Catholic priest

Huy and I share something in common: we are both Tigers according to the Chinese zodiac. Based on Chinese horoscopes, two Tigers are usually not compatible. Tigers are born leaders, respected for their courage, and stand up for what they think is right. Tigers are magnetic and have a natural air of authority. Tigers are tempestuous yet calm, warm-hearted yet fearsome. Tigers love adventures and are always in a hurry to get things done right. Tigers are hard-working, so they accomplish tasks with enthusiasm and efficiency. Tigers make money, but they are not directly interested in money. Tigers are sensitive and emotional. They are capable of great love but can become too intense about it.[1]

Although Huy was not the obvious leader in my family when we were growing up, he has demonstrated leadership skills in everything he has done. He was often overshadowed by Hien, who was ordained as a Catholic priest ten years before Huy was. Huy established the Eucharistic Youth Group at La Purisima Catholic Church in Orange, California, in the mid-1980s, and it is still strong today. He was a soloist for the Vietnamese choir at La Purisima Catholic Church. He taught himself how to play the guitar and keyboard, then later used these skills to compose Vietnamese gospel music. He led a charity project by Cung Tram Productions to produce multiple Vietnamese Gospel albums entitled Bao La Tinh Ngai, roughly translated as His Great Love. The revenue from this project provided support to orphanages in Southeast Asia, religious institutions, and various other charitable causes.

---

1   paraphrased from Chinese-Astrology.co.uk

Huy graduated from Cal State Long Beach and worked for Parker-Hannifin as a computer programmer for about one year. During his college years, his education was interrupted by a sports-related injury. He had paralysis and loss of muscle mass in one leg. He was unable to walk for many years, and no physician could offer any treatment. One day, my mom heard through a relative about an alternative healer in San Jose, California. This lady used methods similar to those of Oriental medicine to provide healing. She eventually gave Huy the strength back in his leg. He regained all his muscle mass and finally walked after many years of being mostly bedridden. I often reflect on what happened to Huy and what has transpired in his life after he was healed. I think God led him to "the healer" so that he can use his talents and leadership skills to serve God and His people. This was his God-given second chance at a more fulfilling life but Huy also let God define what "fulfilling" meant.

People often ask me why Huy left a good job at Parker-Hannifin to join the seminary in his thirties. Why did he not get married and have kids like other men his age? He dated a few ladies in his lifetime, but I don't think he will ever love another woman as much as he loves our mom. I think he made the right decision because he was born a tiger; he is capable of great love that needs to be shared with many so that it does not become too intense. He has demonstrated time and again that he is a "born leader," so he needed to use that talent to best serve the community. Like the tiger, he has the ability to make a lot of money, but to this day he has never been really interested in it. He is always thinking of ways he can give money away. For all these reasons and more, I admire my brother Huy and think of him often in many decisions that I make.

* * *

Hoai Viet "Derek" Nguyen
Born March 1, 1978, in New Orleans, Louisiana
Education: BS in marketing management from California State Polytechnic University, Pomona
Profession: marketing and sales

Derek and I were not very close growing up. He knows I am the strict disciplinarian who would tell my parents if he broke the rules when my parents were away. At the same time, he knows deep down that I only told my parents because I cared about him. My mom had a difficult time dealing with Derek as a teenager and young adult. Mom prayed incessantly for him to change as he went through many stages of rebellion. My mom was at times worried that Derek would lose his religion.

Derek took longer than usual to graduate from college due to changing his major. Once he finished college, he landed various jobs, but struggled for a while to find the right niche. He has spent most of his career in marketing and sales. I am happy to say that in addition to being financially stable, he met the love of his life and got married on February 7, 2015.

What I learned from Derek is to never give up on anyone. Change will come when we persistently pray. Again, my family's faith was strengthened as we gradually saw that through prayer, God can work miracles when we are about to give up. I admire that Derek was receptive to our advice to improve his career and relationships with everyone in the family.

My Sisters

From left, Hanh (Mylene), me, Bich-Ha Pauline, and Thu-Hang Tatiana. We were all wearing red ao dai *at our brother Huy's ordination to the priesthood in 1995.*

Huong Xuan Nguyen
Born November 13, 1964, in Vietnam
Education: attended California State University, Long Beach
Profession: payroll specialist

In my opinion, Huong is the female equivalent of Tuan. Our family members constantly feel the need to be protective of her. She has been the traditional subservient Vietnamese wife and has been in that role religiously since the time she met her husband. She got married at the age of twenty-two and is the only one in our family to have never graduated from college. She got engaged after less than one year of dating her husband. She has delicately balanced love for her husband and love for her children. She has weathered many storms and I admire her for tirelessly working to keep her family together.

In my opinion, of all my siblings Huong has been through the most adversity. In 1984, she was trying to be helpful to a co-worker by giving her a ride home. Huong got into a car accident and was in a coma for more than one week. My family thought we lost her, but God said it was not her time yet. Unfortunately for Huong, the friend who she gave a ride to ended up suing her for bodily injuries. The accident was Huong's fault, so she also faced lawsuits from two other parties. It was a harrowing experience for my family both personally and financially, but God got all of us through that difficult time.

After Huong got married, she had a total of five children and suffered one miscarriage. Huong constantly struggles to strike a balance between loving her husband and nurturing her relationships with her children. She prays often for harmony in the home. Eventually God answered her prayers. Huong now can look forward to all her kids being home for special occasions.

One thing I reflect on often is that God will not put us in situations He knows we cannot handle. I think Huong was placed in these challenging situations because God knew she was a prayerful person and she would seek His guidance to help her through anything. I admire her for her strong faith in God, something I still work on every day.

*   *   *

Thuy-Hong Tiffany Nguyen
Born March 1, 1968, in Vietnam
Education: BA in business administration from California State University, Fullerton
Profession: financial analyst

Hong is the "do-er" in the family. She analyzes every circumstance and thinks of what she can do to help. She doesn't like to sit around and be idle. Throughout my life, that's what I've remembered about Hong. She continues to be that way with her husband and kids. My siblings often have to remind her that she needs to let her husband and kids take care of a few things so that she can take a break after a long week at work. She reminds me of Martha in the Bible: when Jesus was visiting the two sisters, Martha was worried about getting the house ready and serving Jesus rather than listening to His preaching. Hong tends to worry about everyone else's comfort instead of her own.

She is a very involved mom and makes every effort to be a part of any event in her children's lives. She even invites our family members to be a part of those events, and she tries her best to create a strong bond between her children and our family. Hong would drive from Arizona to California just for a one-day family event. She emphasizes that family is the most important thing in her life.

Hong is very religious and the only girl in the family who contemplated becoming a nun. She tried staying at a convent for a few days or so, but eventually had the calling for married life. Although she did not become a nun, she is probably the most devout Catholic of all the girls in our family.

She fasts and abstains from meat on the weekends, tries to go to church more than once a week, and recites prayers of Divine Mercy every afternoon. Even as she incorporates these devout practices routinely into her schedule, she is a working mom, an accountant for pharmaceutical and healthcare companies through most of her career. She later left the corporate world and worked for a Catholic high school in Arizona. She does not impose her religious beliefs on others but will pray for co-workers who are going through difficult times. It has gotten to the point where her coworkers would ask her to pray for them because they saw how many times their difficult decisions were made clear after Hong prayed for them. I have not been blessed with motherhood, but if I ever do, I know that I will look to Hong for advice on how to make everything happen for my children.

*   *   *

Bich-Ha Pauline Nguyen
Born July 29, 1969, in Vietnam
Education: DMD from Tufts University
Profession: dentist

Like Hien, Pauline is a rooster in the Chinese zodiac, and she is very observant and skeptical. She is a straight-shooter and speaks her mind. There's no guessing what she thinks; what you see is what you get. She has a very keen "sixth sense" about situations and about people. Probably because of these traits, my family often turns to Pauline for problem-solving. Sometimes Pauline's suggestions to re-solve conflicts may not agree with my brothers' ideas. However, this often creates opportunities for debate, and in the end it gives everyone multiple perspectives on the same issues. We learn to be better listeners and respect differing points of view, which helps us to come to a reasonable solution for many issues we face together.

Pauline is very simple about appearances, unlike what is said about roosters. From the spartan style of her home decor to her sense of fashion, she reflects how beauty can be very simple and natural. This does not mean she doesn't care about money or possessions. She will be the first to say she loves a bargain and will return something if she finds the same item for even less than a dollar cheaper. She loves playing the scratch lotto and tends to have much more luck than anyone else I know. There were times she would call me and tell me that she won some small amount of money every week playing scratch lotto. She would even park her car somewhere, get out of the car, and right there on the ground is either a winning lotto ticket or some cash. She values every penny, earned or won. She is generous but not to the detriment of her own financial success. That is one trait I admire about Pauline. I am still trying to strike that balance in my personal expenditures and charitable contributions.

Pauline paved the way for me and Mylene to understand that it's reasonable to move away from home and pursue higher educational goals. She is the role model to show that she can care for our parents and other family members without living with them every minute of every day. Pauline and her husband John are the most gracious hosts I have ever known. They make every effort to host any family member at any time of the year when anyone wants to visit Massachusetts. They make us feel comfortable during our stays and meet or exceed our needs. Pauline and John took care of me when I stayed with them to study for the USMLE and other board exams. They supported me throughout my career and I will always be grateful for that.

Although I recognize Pauline as one of the problem-solvers in my family, she and I bounce ideas off each other frequently. She calls me when she thinks she may be too straight-forward in conversations with family members. She speaks her mind and it may come off as being hurtful. She would ask me for input on how to give advice to a family member without appearing mean or critical. I find myself not liking confrontation, so I always think that all I can do is suggest and it's up to the other person to accept advice. So Pauline and I strike a balance while trying to resolve family conflicts. She encourages many of us to speak our minds to help others make important decisions.

As Pauline has gotten older and more established in her career, I admire that she has taken a step back from her work to take care of our parents, siblings, nieces, and nephews. She does not hoard her financial success. She also gives of her time to the family such as providing annual dental services to any of us who so desires. I will never have enough courage to treat my family members. I admire that Pauline is so professional and so giving even when, because she is such a straight-shooter, not everyone shows her the appreciation she so rightly deserves.

*   *   *

Thu-Hang Tatiana Nguyen
Born October 9, 1971, in Vietnam
Education: BA in business marketing from California State University, Fullerton
Profession: singer/model

Tatiana is the opposite of Pauline. She is not a natural leader, but she has a magnetic personality because of her social skills and physical attributes. She has been a singer and model since 1994. She majored in business marketing at Cal State Fullerton and found a job at Ricoh Corporation after finishing college, but she found the eight-to-five routine too boring. She had other talents and wanted to pursue them, so she collaborated with Huy on his charity music project by Cung Tram Productions and produced five Vietnamese Gospel albums. Sometime after the second Gospel album was released, she was offered an opportunity to audition with Asia Entertainment Company, based in Southern California. After one audition at a studio, she was offered a contract to sing for them. As part of the contract, there were photo shoots and video productions which gave her opportunities to travel the world. You can find her products under the artist name Thanh Truc.

Tatiana is married to a Vietnamese music composer, Vu Tuan Duc, and they have a son whose hobbies include playing the piano and basketball. Tatiana does not travel much anymore, but she still participates in music shows, photo shoots, and video productions occasionally. She is a freelance artist but is now working full-time doing medical billing. She and her husband also launched YouTube channels to promote new artists and Vietnamese religious music.

When Tatiana was in college, she was approached by a cereal company that was seeking talent on campus to do commercials for them. She asked my mom for permission to pursue this opportunity, but Mom said no. Mom told her to graduate from college first, then she can do anything else she wants. As we often hear, Mom is always right. Tatiana is very thankful that she has a marketing degree to fall back on because her career as an artist cannot last forever.

One thing I admire about Tatiana is that she followed her dreams wherever they took her. She took chances despite the odds. At the same time, unlike many artists, she upheld principles of her Catholic and Vietnamese upbringing when it came to photo shoots and video productions. She kept the communication lines open with Hien and Huy so they could help her pick the right projects offered to her by the entertainment industry. She uses much of her talent for charity work. She is very creative, which is not a common trait in my family, so she is the person we turn to when we need advice on hair, makeup, and fashion.

After my dad's health began to decline, Tatiana took it upon herself to make sure Dad received the appropriate medical care. I am very grateful that Tatiana was there to take Dad to doctor's visits, ER visits, and medical procedures that were needed. She was the "glue" that held our family together during my dad's illness and after his passing. Tatiana reminds all my siblings to forgive and work towards unity, even when we feel broken.

*   *   *

Hanh My "Mylene" Nguyen
Born July 29, 1976, in Guam
Education: BS from University of California, Irvine
Profession: registered dental hygienist

Mylene is my youngest sister, and we were very close growing up. At times, we were dressed like twins, but I considered myself the less photogenic twin. Mylene was the cute one that everyone wanted to dress up in the cuter outfits. She had her hair done more neatly and even when we had the same hairstyle, she always looked better. She was always the more photogenic one with the infectious smile.

I felt awkward in high school—Mylene had more sociable friends while I was part of the "nerdy" crowd. I did science fair projects, Science Olympiad, won the science medallion, got awarded a plaque for 4.0 or above GPA, and was in lots of academic clubs including National Honor Society and California Scholarship Federation. By achieving all of this, I found my own way to be recognized in the crowd of beautiful people who were having fun in high school.

When we both attended the University of California, Irvine majoring in biological sciences, my academic pursuits did not end. Not only was I taking a full load of courses, I began my work in the research lab during my junior year, which was when Mylene started at UC Irvine. To this day, Mylene will tell my sisters that she hated it when she would barely pass a class and I would say how much I loved that class or enjoyed listening to that professor. I am glad to say that my competitive edge with her regarding academics did not deter her from pursuing a health professions career. She has been very accomplished as a dental hygienist in Massachusetts, working in private practices and also helping Pauline whenever she has some free time.

Mylene and I have a healthy form of sibling rivalry. We went to the same elementary school, high school, and college. She didn't go to medical school but spent a month with me in St. Maarten during my first semester at the American University of the Caribbean School of Medicine. Her playful nature worried me during that stay, but I have learned to trust that my sister has a good head on her shoulders. She has found the love of her life and got married on October 17, 2014. So who is her husband? His name is Tony Tran, and he is the youngest brother of John Tran, Pauline's husband. Sometimes you spend your whole life searching for love when your soulmate is just a few steps away.

*   *   *

I have often reflected on how powerful the Nguyen sisters have been. In reality, we have been the breadwinners of our families. We grew up not being dependent on anyone to financially support us through school or to provide for us on a daily basis. Because of this work ethic, we feel the need to be financially independent even at the cost of overworking ourselves for the benefit of the family. We don't complain about having fulfilling careers and at the same time do our best to carry out responsibilities as wives. Sometimes, I see my sisters bend over backwards between their jobs and family duties just to make everyone happy. I often wished that the women in the Nguyen family were recognized more frequently for their sacrifices.

Pauline, Mylene, and I have lived away from our family for many years. This has allowed us the ability to nurture an independent way of thinking, which is much more Westernized, yet still embrace our conservative upbringing. We have zero tolerance for any forms of abuse towards our siblings and are constantly the voice of reason for the other sisters when they find themselves experiencing marital discord.

11

Giving Without Judging

"And if you lend to those from whom you expect to receive, what credit is that to you? Even sinners lend to sinners, in order to receive back the same amount." —Luke 6:34

ONE OF THE CHALLENGES THAT people often face in making a decision to help someone is the thought of whether they will get something in return. Because of my Christian upbringing and the influence of my parents and siblings, I have never been concerned about this because I think of the reward in the afterlife that awaits me. Other concerns that might hinder an individual from helping someone is the thought of whether the help provided might be misused, such as wondering if money given to someone in need will just be used to buy drugs. When such thoughts arise, I encourage people to think of other ways that help can be given to prevent misuse. I don't think we should concern ourselves with whether we should offer the help, but if there is a willingness to help then let God guide us to the right way to provide that assistance to others. Let God do the judging and allow yourself to be the instrument to carry out God's will.

So many times in my life, from the time I was in college until the present day, I allowed myself to be open to God's calling for me to serve others in unusual circumstances. I had to trust that God put me where I was supposed to be at certain places and gave me the free will to choose whether I would choose to help someone get out of their mess.

> *Let God do the judging and allow yourself to be the instrument to carry out God's will.*

Western Service Workers Association, Santa Ana, California

Sometime between graduating from college and beginning medical school, I was looking for ways to help low income families and underprivileged kids. I came across Western Service Workers Association and spoke to a lady named Jamie. She informed me that many of the families she helped rarely had enough resources to give their kids holiday parties or gifts, and many of them just barely made ends meet each month. This spoke to me, as my family had been in similar circumstances during our first few years in the United States as refugees who came from a war-torn country and spoke very little English. My siblings and I experienced many Christmases where getting twelve rolls of toilet paper gift-wrapped or a small toy from Santa at Chapman College was considered a happy holiday. I felt a tugging in my heart to brighten the holidays for these underprivileged kids.

So under the guidance of Jamie and alongside my younger sister Mylene and many youth groups at La Purisima Catholic Church in Orange, California, we set out to make special holiday meals and bring presents for these kids whenever we could afford it. Just to see the children's smiles and the tears of joy on their parents' faces was the most rewarding experience of this early volunteer work that I led with my friends from the local Catholic church. That was the first time in my life that I recognized I truly had compassion for the poor, but I had to practice it more often in order to awaken other people to a life of service as well.

Volunteering at Western Medical Center, Santa Ana, California

People have often asked me if I always knew I wanted to be a doctor. Nobody in my family was a physician so I had to carve my own path to see what suited my desires and abilities. As I previously mentioned, during my junior year in college I decided to take a research course for credits by working in a research lab with pathologist Dr. Edward R. Arquilla, later working part-time as a research assistant. Dr. Arquilla was both an MD and a PhD, so he cared for patients and conducted laboratory research that was well funded by renowned organizations. I asked Dr. Arquilla, if he could do it all over again, would he study for the MD or PhD program? Surprisingly, he quickly said he would focus on earning his MD only. He told me that science and healthcare had changed so much that physicians could also do research if they so desired. I knew after working in the research lab that I missed human contact. That's when I decided to focus on pursuing medical school.

But did I really know what I was getting into? I decided to call local hospitals to look for volunteer opportunities for college students. I landed a volunteer position first at the emergency room at Western Medical Center in Santa Ana and volunteered there on Saturdays, usually from late afternoon until midnight. I saw the fast-paced nature of patient encounters and the many traumas and codes that happened. After six months in the ER, I knew I wanted to experience a volunteer opportunity to work with children of any age but to see more continuity of care—following a patient from admission to discharge. For the next two years I chose to volunteer every Saturday in the neonatal intensive care unit at Western Medical Center. That was the most amazing experience I had in college before starting medical school. It solidified my commitment to pursuing a career in medicine, and I was quite certain by then that I would want to eventually care for children.

This volunteer experience taught me an important lesson. Sometimes, by giving our time to others, we are given an opportunity to learn more about ourselves, which in turn will give clarity to our purpose in life. This is why when people tell me they don't know if they want to pursue a certain career, I always encourage them to go volunteer in that field for at least a few months before making a lifetime commitment.

Residency Training in Columbia, Missouri, 2002–2006

Hurricane Katrina happened during my residency in Missouri. Because many people were displaced from their homes due to the hurricane, the American Red Cross was asking for help to provide shelter to these people. I donated money and sent in my name to offer a place for anyone displaced from the hurricane. Although I never got a call from the American Red Cross about my offer for shelter, there were medical students and medical residents who wanted to do rotations at Mizzou but didn't have housing. Since I owned a three-bedroom, two-bath ranch-style home and lived there alone, I took in students and residents. I knew how tough it was to make ends meet as a medical student—I remember living off student loans and just hoping I had enough to make it until the next loan check came. I decided not to ask any of the students or residents to pay rent but just contribute to the cost of utilities. I told them I appreciated their company, which allowed me to have dinner with someone every night. I also told them I wanted to help them since many people helped me during my years as a student.. One couple that stayed with me gave me a wedding album, and a resident made me paella for dinner before moving out. I appreciated their tokens of gratitude, but I would do it again without expecting anything in return.

I look back at this time and I often wonder what ever happened to these students and residents. I wondered what specialties they pursued, if they got married and had kids, and what other wonderful things they have accomplished for themselves and their communities. Whatever successes they have achieved, I am just grateful to know that somewhere out there, a few physicians are making a difference for others because I helped them when they were in need.

Spinal Muscular Atrophy (SMA) Eat 'n Run Events, 2010–2014

I didn't know much about spinal muscular atrophy when I met the Merriken family in 2009. Kari Merriken brought her son Caleb to me for a second opinion after seeing many specialists at a hospital in Atlanta. He had feeding difficulties and swallowing problems. He was not growing and he had regressed in his developmental milestones, such as losing the ability to sit and crawl. As a mom, Kari knew something was wrong and she needed to find the right doctors to determine his diagnosis. On his first visit with me, I admitted Caleb to the hospital and started nasogastric tube feeding to help him gain weight. My goal was to see if I could give him some strength by providing nutrition that required little effort from him. I received a call from the American Red Cross the same afternoon Caleb was admitted. I found out that Caleb's father, Kanaan, was a U.S. Army Ranger who was stationed in the Middle East, and the American Red Cross wanted to know if Caleb's condition was life-threatening and if Kanaan needed to come home. I advised that Kanaan should come home because I was still working with other medical experts to figure out Caleb's diagnosis. The American Red Cross allowed Kanaan to come home to be with his son and wife until a diagnosis and treatment plan was determined.

Caleb was hospitalized for over one week for nasogastric tube feeding but never needed a gastrostomy tube, which is more invasive and goes through the abdomen directly into the stomach. He started to eat and drink better as he regained strength. He received therapies as he continued to grow and develop. He did become wheelchair-bound beginning in his toddler years and required treatments for respiratory illnesses more frequently as he got older due to his SMA. Marconi and I were able to attend four years of SMA Eat 'n Run events every March until 2014. At these events I was honored to be a speaker, and I helped with fundraising and took part in a 5K walk along with Marconi and some nurses from MCG. We loved seeing Caleb and the Merriken family members each time we visited Columbus, Georgia.

The Merriken family taught me to get comfortable with caring for special needs children and to have sympathy for the family's challenges. They showed me that if a person is passionate about a cause, she can make anything happen. The Merriken family raised awareness about SMA not only in Georgia but across many other states, and they helped raise money to find treatments for SMA. I am happy to say that as of 2019, there are at least a handful of drugs available for treatment of SMA thanks to the Merriken family. The family has also championed screening for SMA in newborns, something that has been implemented in many states across the country. As for Caleb, he will be twelve years old this year, and he is thriving. His sister also carries the gene for SMA, but thanks to medications she is not showing any symptoms.

Kirkland, Illinois Tornado

One of my goals when I started medical school was to one day establish a nonprofit organization, and I really thought that it would be focused on making a difference in hunger and poverty. When I established Faithful-2-Fitness, I was concerned that I would not have an opportunity to make an impact on poverty and hunger. I prayed often to make sure I was listening to God's calling for me.

About one week before I launched the first program for Faithful-2-Fitness on April 18, 2015, there was a tornado that devastated the Kirkland, Illinois area. The Martinez family had signed up to participate in the first program, and they showed up as often as they could to the classes, but it was challenging because their home and cars were demolished. They didn't even have a roof under which to store the belongings that they were able to salvage after the tornado had passed.

At the end of one of the exercise classes, the mother came to me and shared their family's story. They were still waiting for an insurance assessment in order to get money for a car and a place to stay. In the meantime, they needed a roof to cover a shed that survived the tornado. If they could get money to have a roof installed over the shed, they could store their salvaged belongings safely. I asked the mother how much it would cost for the roof to be installed over the shed, and she told me $200. After hearing her story and reading an article about the tornado devastation, I wrote a $200 check so that the family would have a safe place to store their belongings until their house could be rebuilt. I believe that God put me in touch with the Martinez family to see if I would help them get through that tragic event. Once again, I chose to listen to Him and I saw how my nonprofit work led me to an opportunity to make a difference in poverty and hunger.

Food-4-Fuel

I believe that there's always a reason for everything that happens because of Divine intervention. We may not understand why at the time it happens, but God will reveal His purpose if our hearts are open to seeing it. My encounter with Food-4-Fuel is one of those interesting stories. Back in 2014, when I was looking for a culinary partner for Faithful-2-Fitness, I was so grateful for Jim McIlroy's collaboration with me. Jim came on board right away to help me get connected to many businesses and people in Rockford who have a similar passion for helping the community get healthier. At the time I first met Jim, Food-4-Fuel seemed to be doing fine and he was financially stable. However, about a year later he and his business struggled a bit. That's when I felt a tugging in my heart to help Jim. It was my way of saying thank you for supporting Faithful-2-Fitness. Jim very frequently tells me that he will forever be grateful for the assistance I provided: a loan to keep his business afloat when no bank was able to help him. I just think that God has blessed me with many treasures, so I should use my blessing to help others who are less fortunate than me. I always tell people to think about paying it forward when they are capable.

One thing that I am happy to see is that my decision to help Jim and his family get through a financially challenging time has allowed Jim to pay it forward to numerous organizations in Rockford and the surrounding communities. Jim has partnered with many businesses, nonprofits, and individuals to make a difference in the lives of various people. He continues to have a positive impact on the lives of the homeless, veterans, low-income families, people struggling with mental health problems and addiction, at-risk youth, and many more. Despite the long days he puts in to keep his business running and helping so many people, he remains a dedicated husband and father to three children. Jim is a wonderful partner for my nonprofit organization and a true inspiration for me and many people in the Rockford region.

Nurse Stephanie

When I joined Rockford Memorial Hospital in July 2013, one of the medical assistants who worked with me was Stephanie. She was a single mother with two children, and she had suffered from unfaithful and abusive relationships. She was studying to become a nurse so that she could get out of a cycle of dependency on a partner or the government for financial assistance. She was renting and had to move many times over three or four years due to challenges with making ends meet with expenses like rent, utilities, and tuition for nursing school or for her kids to attend private school.

A few times during nursing school, she periodically reunited with the father of her youngest child, even though he was verbally and physically abusive. She struggled to make ends meet because he was not paying child support. She didn't have money to buy a laptop for nursing school, so I loaned her my extra laptop. At times, she either couldn't pay the electric bill or was at risk of being homeless because she couldn't pay rent on time. At one point, she thought about dropping out of nursing school because she couldn't afford the next semester's tuition. Through the many times she struggled financially, I knew God put me in Stephanie's life so that I had to choose if I was going to help her get out of her mess. I chose to pay as often as I could to make sure she and her kids were not homeless and that she would accomplish her goals. I am happy to say that Stephanie graduated from nursing school and currently works as an ER nurse in Rockford.

Although Stephanie and I no longer work together, she will periodically send me texts asking for prayers. I had given her a prayer card so that she could pray to her guardian angel. I remind her to pray for guidance through times of trouble and know that I am only a phone call away. She often tells me she doesn't know how she will ever repay me. I've told her to pay it forward by helping others in her role as an ER nurse, and to use her time or talent to help others, even if she doesn't have treasures. My experience with Stephanie reminds me to help people whenever I am capable because I might be the one that God is sending to answer their prayers.

Rockford Blessing Bags for the Homeless, November and December 2016–2018

At the beginning of Advent in 2016, I was sitting in church during Sunday Mass and the priest was talking about ways to make this Advent more memorable than any other. On my way home, I kept thinking about ways I could make life better for homeless people. I logged onto Facebook as usual to check messages and posts. All of a sudden, I saw a post from my friend Jim McIlroy about wanting to do something for the homeless in Rockford. He shared a video of a young man videotaping homeless people telling him what they wanted for the holidays. After making the videos, this person purchased what the homeless people wanted and personally delivered the items to them.

That video inspired me to read further for other ideas to help the homeless. I came across an article of a mother and daughter in Arizona who made blessing bags to give out to the homeless. I researched things that were helpful for the homeless to have that most of us take for granted—nonperishable food, socks, gloves, scarves, and hygiene/toiletry items. From this inspiration, Jim McIlroy and I recruited volunteers and asked for donations to make blessing bags for the homeless and poor in Rockford. These blessing bags included things like nonperishable food, water, candies, cookies, socks, gloves, scarves, toiletries and first aid supplies. This project brought together people of all ages from different races and socioeconomic backgrounds, working together to make a difference for those in need, especially during the holidays. It's just our small way of saying we care and will share our blessings with others as a way of thanking God for our blessings each day.

Martin Luther King, Jr. Day, January 16, 2017

My faith community meets at my house on Tuesday nights, and one of the questions we often share is "Where did you see God this week?"

I was leaving work on the evening of Martin Luther King, Jr. Day in 2017. As I was waiting to make a left turn at the stop sign on Rockton Avenue to leave Rockford Memorial Hospital, from the corner of my eye I saw two people walking through the rain to the passenger side of my car. As they approached, I saw a mother and her approximately ten-year-old daughter holding onto each other to avoid slipping on the ice. The mother was desperately signaling for me to roll down my window. For a few seconds, I wondered whether I should or not, worried about being harmed. However, it didn't take long for me to roll down the passenger window.

The mom then asked me if I was traveling towards State Street. Without hesitation, I told the mom and daughter to hop into the back seat. They were soaking wet in their jackets. The mom asked me if I could drive them to "the Mission." I said I didn't know where "the Mission" was, so I asked for the address and then punched it into my GPS. I began driving towards "the Mission," not having any idea where I was actually going in this rainy weather on the slick roads.

As I drove, they introduced themselves and told me that the daughter had an appointment with her doctor for diabetes and celiac disease. They tried to catch the city bus but waited for forty-five minutes without seeing one. There had been freezing rain most of the day, and it rained harder while they waited. They were desperate for help, so when they saw my car, they decided to take a chance and ask. During the fifteen-minute drive, I found out that she was a single mother living in a shelter with her daughter. Mom was waiting on her ex-husband to pay child support ($133 per month). In the meantime, she was getting training to develop skills to land a job to support her daughter.

I told her that I was a parishioner at Holy Family Catholic Church and served on the fundraising committee for St. Vincent de Paul Society, which helps the poor in Rockford. I encouraged her to contact the church to get help from the society.

This incident touched my heart tremendously for weeks, and I even shared my story on social media. I wanted to encourage people to take notice of our friends in need. I pray every day that I am grateful for what I have and to be granted opportunities to help those less fortunate than I am. I believe that God brought these two people to me that night to see if I would see Him in them.

Hurricane Irma in St. Maarten

In September 2017, Hurricane Irma, a category 5 storm, hit the island of St. Maarten and caused massive devastation. The American University of the Caribbean School of Medicine in St. Maarten was built to withstand a category 5 hurricane, and it had its own generator to supply electricity in emergencies. However, because of the extensive devastation to the rest of the island, the medical students were forced to evacuate and relocate to Chicago or England to complete the remaining semester of medical school until the island could be rebuilt and be inhabitable again. I empathize with the medical students and the people of St. Maarten because I had weathered three hurricanes while attending medical school on that island. However, I was fortunate to not be forced to evacuate despite the storms at that time. As a way to show support for the people of St. Maarten and the medical students at AUC School of Medicine, I joined efforts to contribute to a GoFundMe page for St. Maarten Hurricane Irma recovery efforts. It was my small way of saying thank you to St. Maarten for being the wonderful place where my medical career began. It warmed my heart to see so many alumni coming together to make a difference for the students and the island of St. Maarten.

January 2018—Donation for Dominican Republic Mission Trip

One of my goals not yet achieved is to contribute my time to a mission trip in a developing country. I had actually interviewed for Doctors Without Borders in 2012 and was accepted to be part of the organization. However, due to a minimum six-month commitment for my first assignment, I was unable to accept this opportunity. I feel that when it's my time to do something like this, God will open up doors for me to follow that path.

In January 2018, I saw a Facebook post from the McIlroy family asking to support their children on a mission trip to the Dominican Republic. I felt called to support their children, knowing that this was my way to contribute my treasures, allowing them to volunteer their time to serve low-income families in the Dominican Republic. The experience on the mission trip helped the McIlroy kids build more confidence in themselves, and they discovered compassion for those with limited access to food, water, and healthcare resources. I was delighted to see what a positive impact the mission trip had on the kids. Although I have not directly given my time to this cause, God blessed me with treasures in order to make a difference in the lives of the families in the Dominican Republic as well as the McIlroy family.

St. Vincent de Paul Society in Rockford, Illinois

In 2017, Holy Family Catholic Church formed the first St. Vincent de Paul conference in Rockford, and our pastor invited parishioners to contribute time and talent to serve on the committees. It was a difficult decision for me to consider adding another church activity to my already busy work schedule. It meant I had to go to more evening meetings after work and devote time to serve in various capacities. I had a passion to serve the poor and needy, so after much prayer I decided to join the fundraising committee. I knew that I had the ability to personally contribute to fundraisers and invite others to donate in some way to our events. Although I was on the fundraising committee, I found that I was able to engage many friends and co-workers to contribute to St. Vincent de Paul by donating many household items, furniture, clothing, and various other necessities to help the poor in the Rockford region. I used my experience with organizing my 5K events for Faithful-2-Fitness to help with the annual Friends of the Poor Walk. Even when I couldn't attend the Applebee's Flapjack (all-you-can-eat pancakes) fundraising event, I bought tickets and gave them out to kids, single mothers, and low-income families so they could go enjoy some pancakes. It was also my way of letting the public know more about the work of St. Vincent de Paul Society.

Although I initially hesitated about whether I wanted to be a part of St. Vincent de Paul Society, I realized in 2018 how much the group meant to me. My father passed away on April 2, 2018. Once the group learned about my father's passing, many messages of condolences, encouragement, and support from fellow members helped me get through a difficult time. I found my niche to volunteer my time, talent, and treasure to help the poor in Rockford. In December 2018, I felt called to help St. Vincent de Paul by making a $5,000 donation to the conference in memory of my father, Peter Hau Van Nguyen. I felt called by my father's soul to honor him by helping St. Vincent de Paul Society in Rockford. Not only did this donation help me heal during a time of grief, it also allowed me to continue honoring my father long after he had left this world to seek eternal life with the Lord.

Uncle Tien

Uncle Tien is my dad's youngest sibling. Ever since the mid-'70s when my family arrived in the United States, my uncle has squandered his opportunity to pursue an education as a pathway to a brighter future. Early on, he worked odd jobs and used his money to gamble. He would lie to my family and relatives about his whereabouts and borrowed money from people by using our family's name, since we were held with great esteem in the community. My family would only find out years later that he had accumulated so much debt from borrowing money and gambling. He would go through cycles of highs and lows, reappearing in our lives whenever he needed us. He had deceived my family and many relatives. He had lost our trust and burned so many bridges. Even when he seemed to have a conversion of heart, he would eventually go back to his old ways.

After my father passed away in 2018, I felt the need to find my uncle in order to tell him what had happened. My dad had asked a lot about Uncle Tien in the months leading up to his passing. I hoped that my uncle would change after hearing that my dad was gone. I also hoped that my dad's soul could guide my uncle towards a more righteous path. Soon after my dad passed away, I made phone calls to a homeless shelter in Las Vegas where my uncle had previously sought help, but the case workers there said they had not seen him check in recently.

Eventually, I called the Las Vegas Police Department to ask about how to file a missing person's report. At that point, I just wanted to know if my uncle was still alive. I called the local jails and there was no evidence that my uncle committed any crimes. I was directed back to the police department and gave enough information to file a missing person's report. On my dad's 100-day memorial service, while I was standing next to my dad's grave, I received a call from the Las Vegas Police Department letting me know that my uncle had been found at the homeless shelter. I shed tears of joy and couldn't wait to let my family know.

That night, I shared the news about my uncle with my family members. Incidentally, that day was July 11, which also marked Tien's daughter's sixteenth birthday. I told my family that if we are to live the Gospel's message, then we need to bring back the one sheep that is lost. Not all my family members agreed, but I stuck to my conviction to see it through to save my uncle, not just spiritually but in practical ways as well.

During the summer and fall of that year, I took time to listen to my family and pray for guidance on what to do about Uncle Tien. At Thanksgiving, my husband and I decided to fly to Las Vegas to pick up my uncle from the homeless shelter. I met with several administrators of the homeless shelter, which was run by Catholic Charities of Southern Nevada. As a way to say thank you for helping my uncle, I wrote a check for $5,000 to give back to the shelter. It warmed my heart to be able to do something for those less fortunate during Thanksgiving that year. I felt my dad's spirit during that visit at the shelter and I knew he would be proud of what I did for my uncle and for the homeless shelter.

Uncle Tien spent a couple of days in Las Vegas dining elaborately with us and attending a Cirque du Soleil show featuring the music of Michael Jackson. After our time in Vegas, I rode the Megabus with my uncle to Anaheim, California, where we visited my dad at his gravesite. I arranged for my uncle to reunite with his daughter over dinner with me and my sister Tatiana, and he spent the Thanksgiving holiday with some of my family members. It was very heartbreaking for me to let him go back to the homeless shelter in Las Vegas after spending one week with him. My sisters and I provided our uncle with warm clothes, plenty of snacks, some money, and gift cards to help for a few months. I had this fear that he would go back to gambling, but I had to give him a chance to figure out his goals for the rest of his life. I wasn't sure if he was ready to leave his homeless life behind.

During the time I was able to spend with my uncle, he shared stories of his life as a homeless person. He said that there were nights he couldn't get a bed at the shelter despite waiting for hours. He would try to find safe places to sleep or keep warm, and sometimes he slept at the cemetery on top of tombstones. The police would stop by and ask if he was fine but never told him he had to leave. He feared for his life, worried he would be assaulted or murdered any given night. He also made friends with others who were homeless and didn't get shelter those nights either.

Some nights, he decided to visit the adoration chapel and pray. He often fell asleep while at chapel and was discovered by others attending chapel. Sometimes he would be asked by other adorers at the chapel if he needed anything. Other times, he was kicked out of the chapel because people found out he was homeless.

There were times that he was able to beg for a few bucks while sitting on the streets. He used the money to buy a bus pass that allowed him unlimited rides. This gave him a way to stay warm while sitting on the bus sleeping all night. However, there were times where he had to get off the bus and change to other buses because the drivers did not want homeless people staying on the same bus all night.

He also admitted that at times he misused people's generosity. He would collect money from people passing by and then use it to gamble at the casinos. Sometimes he won big, but then his addiction led him to gamble all of it away. He gambled without prioritizing his hunger, sleep, or God. He was lost chasing that high and hoping for an easy way out of his homelessness and poverty.

Even after knowing all of these details about my uncle, I chose to love him as a child of God and to forgive him as often as needed as long as I could save his soul at the end of his life. I told him that God does not give up on him, so I won't give up on him. I prayed to my dad's soul to intercede for my uncle's true conversion. I had to trust that I had done my best and allow God to take care of everything from there.

Around February 2019, my uncle called me to say he had run out of money for bus passes. He said he had been going to church daily except Saturdays. He was still staying at the homeless shelter, but because of the government shutdown at the time, he didn't get food stamps for February and might not for March either. He had access to healthcare through Medicaid, but that was only good until September 2019. With all these challenges in his life, he asked me what goals I had for him. I told him that I don't set goals for anyone, but I could help a person achieve goals by providing guidance and financial assistance. My sisters also spoke to him with the same message. Ultimately, we all told my uncle that he had to show us he was a truly changed man by finding a job and a place to live.

A few weeks later, I was on vacation in Florida for my birthday, and the first place I stopped was St. Augustine, which I later learned was where the first Catholic parish in the United States was formed. I visited Mission Nombre de Dios, the location of where the first Catholic parish Mass was celebrated in the United States, and I prayed at the adoration chapel at the Shrine of Our Lady of La

Leche. One of my prayer requests was for my uncle to turn away from gambling and toward God's path for him.

On my last day of vacation, I received a text from Uncle Tien. He told me that a man approached him after Mass the week before, asking him if he was okay. My uncle told the man that he was not okay, that he was looking for a place to live and wanted to get a job. This man took my uncle under his wing and moved him into his home on March 1, 2019, the Friday before the start of Lent. The man trained my uncle in landscaping and machine shop skills. Once my uncle completed training, he would be paid for the work he would do for this man and would be allowed to live in this man's home with a private room and bath, plus utilities and food, all for $400 per month. I wrote a card and mailed a check to this man, thanking him for being the answer to my prayers for God to send a "St. Ambrose" to help my uncle out of his gambling addiction. I thanked the man via text messages for all the help he had provided my uncle. I continued to pray that no matter how many times my uncle may fail, there will always be someone in his life to guide him along the path towards true conversion.

St. Augustine of Hippo spent many years of his life in wicked living and false beliefs. He was an intelligent man brought up a Christian, but his sins of impurity and pride darkened his mind so much he could not see or understand the Divine Truth anymore. Through the prayer of his mother St. Monica and the preaching of **St. Ambrose**, St. Augustine finally became convinced that Christianity was the one true religion.

I am realistic and know that even people of faith understand that addiction of any kind is a constant battle. I had asked Uncle Tien to surrender his addiction, strengths, and weaknesses to God. Only with true surrender to God and asking Him for help to remain on the path to true conversion will he be able to become a forever-changed person. Despite my pleading, my uncle only lasted about one or two weeks after moving in with the family before going back to gambling. I had sent the owner of the house a check to pay for my uncle's rent. Somehow, my uncle convinced the man to cash the check and give him the money directly. To this day, I still don't understand how he was able to manipulate the man to do that. After that, Uncle Tien admitted to me that he had gone to the casino and gambled all the money away, and he was forced to move back to the homeless shelter. I was very upset about what my uncle did; it was a total betrayal of my love and trust. I took some time to heal my heart and forgive my uncle, while giving him space to decide what he wanted to do with his life, before I got back in touch with him.

Around May 2019, my uncle texted me and asked to talk to me when I was free. At first, I was hesitant about responding to his text message, because I wanted to protect myself from being hurt again. After praying about this and asking my dad to help me, I decided to call my uncle that afternoon. We talked and he told me he had been staying at the homeless shelter, but he was also being paid for doing odd jobs such as yard work. He was able to save up $300 and decided to look for a room to rent. He found one listed in the newspaper for $250 per month, furnished with a bed, TV, and small refrigerator. The room was part of a bigger home owned by a Vietnamese widow named Cathey. Interestingly, she was also a refugee who had lived in Guam, just like my family did after escaping from Vietnam. After speaking to Cathey and confirming that my uncle had moved in and paid the rent for May, I decided to help him once again.

Uncle Tien asked me to help him with June and July rent while he continued to apply for jobs that could offer him more regular hours, more tolerable work conditions for his age, and possibly health insurance. I mailed checks to Cathey to cover June and July rent for my uncle, and I sent him a large box of nonperishable food and gift cards. It was my small way to feed my uncle until he made enough money to feed himself, and to show him I cared. While waiting for the shipment to arrive at my uncle's place, I ordered pizza the next night from Papa John's in Las Vegas and had it delivered so that he would have dinner for a few days. I wanted to first feed him physically so that I would be given a chance to nourish him spiritually.

My uncle was offered a position working at Target for a few weekends. He made enough money to pay for groceries, a bus pass, and his phone bill. He interviewed for jobs at a few fast food chains but eventually accepted a full-time job at a golf club. His work place was located near casinos, so my uncle would have to face his temptation to gamble. In the past, he had lived in other places far away from casinos but still managed to find his way to them after he collected his paychecks. I told him that if he could battle his gambling addiction while being surrounded by casinos, then he could battle it anywhere. I encouraged him to pray for God to help him battle his temptations and addictions each day, and I also encouraged him to pray for and to my dad, who is now like our guardian angel. I am grateful that my uncle has been holding his full-time job since July 4, 2019. He has been living in the same place, paying his rent since August 2019 and covering all of his expenses.

Around the end of June 2019, I mailed my uncle a few cards and stamps so that he could write to his daughter in California. I advised him to write to her often and to send her money or gifts as a way to begin rebuilding a relationship with her. He later told me that he had written to his daughter for her birthday on July 11 and again before she started her senior year of high school. His daughter later texted me and thanked me for helping her dad work towards being the man God wants him to be. I told her that my dad has passed away but her dad is still here; that my dad would be very happy watching from above, seeing the changed man that her dad has become. I reassured her that helping her dad was my small way to continue to honor my dad.

When Uncle Tien received his first paycheck, he texted me a copy of his pay stub. I sent him an Edible Arrangements fruit package to congratulate him on this accomplishment and to let him know how proud I was of him. I wanted him to know that I truly cared about all the little steps he was taking to becoming a better man, a better father, and a better Catholic. Towards the end of July, I felt called to send him a few books from one of my favorite authors, Matthew Kelly. I ordered him copies of *Resisting Happiness* and *Rediscover the Saints*, books I felt would feed him spiritually. I wanted him to realize that it's never too late to change. I wanted to remind him of God's mercy and forgiveness. I wanted to reinforce in him that the path to holiness is possible for everyone at any time in their life. I wanted my uncle to use his time on the bus rides to work, on breaks at work, and time on the weekend to read spiritual books like I do. I wanted him to feel free to share with me his struggles in life—addiction, temptations, faith, and the path to true conversion. I wanted him to see that there are people out there struggling like him and there are people like Matthew Kelly who are helping these people towards the path to righteousness. I wanted my uncle to stop resisting happiness and find true happiness by surrendering his entire life to God. Uncle Tien has benefited greatly from reading these books and continues to share with me times that he will re-read certain chapters for inspiration and motivation.

A statement that I like to repeat to my uncle is the following: The difference between a saint and sinner is that the saint keeps on trying. Variations of this statement have been shared by Oscar Wilde, St. Teresa of Calcutta, and St. Josemaría Escrivá. This statement is a great reminder that holiness is possible for everyone.

My uncle is now sixty years old. Some days, it's difficult for him to get up at midnight to get on the 1:30 a.m. bus, arrive at work by 4:00 a.m., and work until

1:00 p.m. He goes to sleep at 5:00 p.m., then wakes up at midnight to start each day again. He gets some Saturdays off but always goes to church on Sundays. He reminds me about Holy Days of Obligation and to pray the Rosary, especially during the month of the Rosary in October. He shares his stories about when he felt my dad helping him get

> *The difference between a saint and sinner is that the saint keeps on trying. This is a great reminder that holiness is possible for everyone.*

through his mornings just to get on the bus. He shares that he reflects on the times he was a terrible husband and father. He prays that his wife and daughter forgive him for his failures. He shares that he has realized that the most important relationship in his life is his relationship with God. All these little conversations we have every few weeks are moments which give me hope that God continues to work on my uncle. I just have to continue to pray for him and allow God to do the rest.

I truly believe that my decision to embrace opportunities to help others throughout my life has come back to bless me, my family, and my uncle. My continued assistance to my uncle is my way to honor my father, because I know my dad would want someone to rescue my uncle out of darkness into God's merciful embrace.

Medical Assistant Christine

I have never been blessed with motherhood, so I admire mothers who are able to do everything for their children, setting aside their own personal needs. I have an even greater admiration for moms who also pursue a career while doing a wonderful job raising their kids. And I have a special place in my heart for single moms who try to do everything without a reliable partner. For this reason, I find myself repeatedly trying to do things for single mothers so I can make their day or their children's day just a little brighter. I feel that it is therapeutic to be able to play a positive role in the lives of other people's children since I don't have children of my own.

There was a medical assistant who came to work in our pediatric gastroenterology practice in 2017. Her name is Christine and she is a single mother with a young boy who has many health issues that require special therapies. The child's father has not been involved in his life, even when offered opportunities to visit, and he has not fulfilled his child support responsibilities. So needless to say, Christine can barely make ends meet each month, even when nothing disastrous happens in her life.

In April 2019, I was taking a trip to California to commemorate my father on the first anniversary of his passing. I was visiting Dad at the cemetery when I received a text message from Christine telling me that the used car she had purchased less than a year ago just broke down on the way to work. She was devastated because her young son was recovering from surgery at the time. He also had sensory issues and was just beginning therapies at the hospital, and she had to file for Family Medical Leave Act (FMLA) leave in order to get time off for his therapy appointments. So to have her car engine die on the way to work was just another challenge that this single mother couldn't take at this time. It would cost her $6,000 to get the car engine replaced, and she still owed a large amount of money on the car, which did not have any warranty coverage. Christine asked me if I knew any charities in Rockford that could help her with getting the car fixed. I had previously referred her to St. Vincent de Paul Society and they helped her pay her electric bill for one month. I asked her to reach out to St. Vincent de Paul Society again, though I didn't have much hope since there was a limit on the amount that St. Vincent de Paul Society could give to an individual within a six-month period. The organization's philosophy is to give a "hand up, not a handout," as St. Vincent de Paul Society does not want to encourage dependency. Not surprisingly, Christine told me a few days later that St. Vincent de Paul Society could not help her this time.

I couldn't let Christine struggle alone because I know she was a hard worker and was doing her best at work and at home raising a special-needs child. Once I returned from California, I posted a message on Facebook asking friends to help Christine. I asked if anyone knew a mechanic that could fix the car at a lower cost and if anyone knew of any dealerships that had reliable cars under $3,000 that I could buy for her. I asked for anyone who could contribute in some way to help Christine during this challenging time.

A few days after I posted this message, a nurse that worked with Christine decided to create a GoFundMe to help Christine. Within one month, we raised $1,110. I decided to match the total donation dollar-for-dollar. I also got another $200 donation from one of my sisters by mail after she saw a link to the GoFundMe on my Facebook page. The generosity of the community was infectious, and in the end Christine received more than $2,000, which was used to begin the payments for her car repairs. In the end she got a brand new engine for her car in less than one month from the time GoFundMe was created. This experience showed me that if only one person cared enough to help someone, that caring could create a ripple effect in the community to help people like Christine who are struggling despite putting their best foot forward every day.

Fatherhood Encouragement Project

When used correctly, social media can bring people together to make a difference rather than create negativity. That's what I've appreciated since signing up for a Facebook account in 2009. Social media has allowed me to keep in touch with people from my past and connect with new friends. I read posts on social media to be inspired and motivated. I seek out opportunities to help those in need. I share messages to inspire other people. I share memories made with family and friends so that I will cherish them in years to come.

On July 6, 2019, while scrolling through Facebook, I noticed a post from the Fatherhood Encouragement Project in Rockford. The message read "KIDS IN NEED—CAN YOU HELP?" There was a graphic showing a picture of a little boy and girl holding hands. The description below the message was as follows: "We have 2 children who desperately need our help. Their mother left them and moved and unfortunately this week their father passed away suddenly and the children are left with nothing. They are in need of the following: the girl is three and the boy is five. I guess the boy is small and wears size 4-5 and size 12 shoes. The girl is 3T. Message us if you can help!"

As I mentioned before, Marconi and I don't have children, but any time I hear about children needing something, there is a tugging in my heart to help however I am capable. Marconi was out of town visiting his family in Georgia and I had the weekend off, so the timing was perfect for me to do something to help these kids. I messaged the Fatherhood Encouragement Project and got in touch with the children's paternal grandmother. We arranged to meet at Cherryvale Mall at a store called The Children's Place. Starting from this store, I was able to take the kids and their grandma on a shopping spree. They got their feet measured to get the right shoes for school. It was wonderful to see these kids smile after experiencing such tragedy.

After we finished shopping for the kids, their grandma sat and talked to me while the kids enjoyed some ice cream. I learned that it was grandma's birthday, and she was going to head over to her daughter's house, where her daughter was cooking dinner for her birthday. I went to Mrs. Fields and bought Grandma a cookie cake that had "Happy Birthday" written on it. This grandma deserved a little pampering, and not just on her birthday. Grandma shared that her son, the father of the kids, died at home suddenly in his thirties of a heart attack. He had just recovered from drug addiction and was getting back on the right track. The mother had many children with different men and decided to just leave all her kids with their fathers or grandparents. It was just so sad to hear the mess that this grandma was facing.

As I sat there listening, I recognized common things that connected the two of us. July 7 was the wedding anniversary of my sister and brother-in-law. July 7 was Grandma's birthday, and I was meeting her on this day. Her son suffered addiction to drugs; my uncle suffered addiction to gambling. Her son died of a heart attack; my dad died of a heart attack. She works at the local fire department; my first job at fourteen years old was at a fire department. We had so many things in common that we talked to each other like we've known one another all our lives. We exchanged phone numbers once again and agreed to keep in touch so that I could continue to provide for the kids any time they needed something. We have continued to text since that meeting at the mall and eventually I sent the kids gift cards and treats for the Christmas holiday. I feel so blessed that God brought us together through the help of social media. Being able to make a difference in these children's lives just makes my heart so full.

12

Why Live to Give

"At the end of our lives, we will not be judged by how many diplomas we have received, how much money we have made, or how many great things we have done. We will be judged by 'I was hungry and you gave me something to eat. I was naked and you clothed me. I was homeless and you took me in.'" —St. Teresa of Calcutta

AN ATTENDING PHYSICIAN ONCE TOLD me, "You can't be professionally happy until you are personally happy." I have spent most of my life searching for that happiness.

One of my favorite authors is Matthew Kelly. He is the founder of Dynamic Catholic and a *New York Times* bestselling author. I had heard of him when I received a free copy of his book *Rediscover Jesus* from Holy Family Catholic Church in Rockford for Christmas 2015. I read that book with my faith community and shared many reflections to help me grow spiritually. I was given a copy of another one of his books, *Resisting Happiness*, on Christmas Eve in 2016 at St. Brigid Catholic Church in Georgia. I was curious about the title; I've been searching for happiness my entire life, so why would I want to read about resisting it? I decided to start reading the book on my flight back to Illinois when Christmas vacation ended. It took me less than one week to read it.

Reading *Resisting Happiness* was one of the best decisions I've made. I saw myself in every chapter of that book, as if Matthew Kelly had been there by my side every day. This book has changed my outlook on my career, the practice of my Catholic faith, and life in general. After I finished reading this book, I ordered twenty-four copies and gave them out to family members, friends, and co-workers.

I wanted to share the message of the book to help others become the best version of themselves, to stop resisting that path to enduring happiness.

Around January 2017, I decided to join the Dynamic Catholic Ambassador's Club as a way to support their work. I realized that the free books given out at churches were made possible by the ambassadors and other private donors. I wanted to help Dynamic Catholic with its mission "to re-energize the Catholic Church in America by developing world-class resources that inspire people to rediscover the genius of Catholicism." By giving a monthly donation of $10, Dynamic Catholic mails me books by Kelly and his collaborating authors. I went on to read *Beautiful Hope*, *Perfectly Yourself*, *Why I Love Being Catholic*, and many more of his prized works. The more I read Kelly's books, the more I asked myself what I was passionate about and what God wanted me to do to become a better version of myself every day.

People have frequently asked me why I feel the need to brighten someone's day, even people I barely know. I often say it's because I don't know if I'll die tomorrow and not get the chance to do more for society. I was inspired by a friend of mine, Rod Pollard, to choose the title *Live to Give* for this book.

Why do I live to give?

I live to give as a way of thanking God for His blessings in my life.

I live to give in order to remind myself to be grateful often.

I live to give as a way to pay it forward in honor of those who have helped me achieve my goals in the past, present, and future.

I live to give because the more that I give to others, the more God will bless me in return.

I live to give in order to create a positive ripple effect in my community and invite others to be charitable along with me.

I live to give because I believe that the good I do for others will come back to me and my loved ones especially when we are most in need.

People may choose to give of their time, talent, or treasures in hopes of getting something in return as a reward while on Earth. Whatever the reason may be, I encourage you to think of ways you can give by using the gifts your Creator has given you. Your act of giving is a noble deed, and the more you practice it the more naturally charitable you will become as you encounter people and situations each day.

I hope that I have inspired you to be open to helping others and encouraging other people to pay it forward. Remember that the positive ripple effect can start with you. Trust in God's purpose for you in this life and have faith that the good you do for another person will be rewarded in your eternal life with Jesus Christ.

About the Author

Kim-Doan Katrina Nguyen is a pediatric gastroenterologist who is currently a *locum tenens* and telemedicine physician. She is a clinical associate professor at the University of Illinois College of Medicine in Rockford.

Dr. Nguyen was nominated for the Leonard Tow Humanism in Medicine Award in 2016 and 2017. In January 2017, she was awarded the Faculty & Staff Aureus Award from the University of Illinois College of Medicine based on nominations from medical students. In October 2018, she was nominated by Mercyhealth for the Crusader Community Health Annual Spirit of Caring Award as one of only seven nominees in the Rockford region for that year.

Dr. Nguyen attends Holy Family Catholic Church in Rockford. She lives with her husband, Marconi, and their dog, Corky the Yorkie, in Loves Park, Illinois.

To learn more about Dr. Nguyen's nonprofit,
Faithful-2-Fitness, visit *www.faithful2fitness.org.*